1 MONTH OF
FREE
READING

at
www.ForgottenBooks.com

By purchasing this book you are eligible for one month membership to ForgottenBooks.com, giving you unlimited access to our entire collection of over 1,000,000 titles via our web site and mobile apps.

To claim your free month visit:

www.forgottenbooks.com/free219778

ISBN 978-0-483-77855-9
PIBN 10219778

For support please visit www.forgottenbooks.com

A SERIES

OF

SEVEN SERMONS

ON THE DOCTRINE OF HOLY SCRIPTURE AND OF THE CHURCH
OF ENGLAND RESPECTING THE

SACRAMENT OF BAPTISM,

THE

RITE OF CONFIRMATION,

AND THE

SACRAMENT OF THE LORD'S SUPPER,

IN THEIR MUTUAL RELATIONS:

PREACHED IN ST. MARY'S, WALTHAMSTOW, IN VIEW OF THE CON-
FIRMATION OF THE YOUNGER MEMBERS OF THE CHURCH
RESIDING IN THAT PARISH.

BY

WILLIAM WILSON, B. D.,

VICAR OF WALTHAMSTOW.

WALTHAMSTOW:

PRINTED FOR AND SOLD BY G. BIRD, WOOD STREET.

1840.

The Reader is requested to make the following.
correction :

Page 106, lines 10, 11, for "Sacraments" read Sacrament.

ADVERTISEMENT.

THE Sermons contained in this volume were not composed with a view to publication. They are printed as they were addressed by the Author to his congregation. Should they, in their present form, minister to the benefit of any of those over whose spiritual interests he has watched, not without anxious and affectionate solicitude, for now more than eighteen years, his most earnest wish in thus submitting them to their perusal will be attained; but he is not without hope that the produce of the sale of them, the whole of which he cheerfully devotes to that object, may serve as the commencement of a fund to be expended both in promoting among the poorer members of one part of his flock, that infant education which these Discourses have incidentally but especially in view to enforce, and also in affording larger facilities for the work of the ministry in a district remote from the parish church.

CONTENTS.

SERMON I.

THE NATURE OF THE

RITE OF CONFIRMATION

IN ITS CONNEXION WITH THE

SACRAMENT OF BAPTISM.

---

2 KINGS xxiii. 3:

And all the people stood to the covenant.

THE circumstances which led to this public renewal
of a profession of faith and obedience on the part of
the Church of God in Judæa, are very simply nar-
rated in the context.

It would appear, that during the course of the corruption of the true worship of God which had been
taking place throughout the reigns of Manasseh and
other apostate kings, diligent search had been made
for all copies of the law of God, whether in the temple or elsewhere, in order that by their destruction
the principal impediment to the universal prevalence
of idolatry might be removed. The gates of hell,
however, did not prevail against the true Church of

B

God. The great principles of that law were still in such measure handed down from one generation to another, that even the wicked were restrained from the open renunciation of the worship of the true God, and the righteous found in them a light, faint as it might be, whereby to guide their doubtful steps, or to direct them in the religious instruction of their children. Meantime some, perhaps mutilated copies or distinct parts, themselves injured and corrupted, would doubtless still be retained. And the context leaves it clear, that in the midst of the general destruction of the copies of the Law, some pious priest had secreted, somewhere within the precincts of the temple, that which had been originally written by the hand of Moses, and from which alone all copies must have derived their correctness and authority.

During the reign of idolatry, this copy was thus lost to the Church. But when the good King Josiah proposed to restore the true worship of God, and, so far as he could make himself acquainted with them, the dominion of those principles of conduct which had been a subject of Divine Revelation, he gave directions for the repair of the neglected temple; and there Hilkiah, the high-priest, in making preparation for the desired work, discovered again the hidden treasure— the copy of the Law which had been written by Moses himself.*

This book of Moses was the record of the covenant which God had made with his people, and in which they had of late been but imperfectly instructed. The

---

* 2 Chron. xxxiv. 14.

King determined to make it the rule of his own conduct, and bearing in mind his obligations to be a nursing father to the Church, he took measures to bring together all the families of the people, " both small and great;" and " he read in their ears all the words of the book of the covenant which was so found in the house of the Lord." To this time, the people had, from adverse circumstances, attained to only an imperfect acquaintance with the terms of the covenant, according to which they had all been devoted to God in their infancy.* Now, the inspired Law is unfolded before them—every word, every blessing and every obligation, is plainly and affectionately stated to them in the words of the Sacred Volume; and what is the result? " All the people," it is said, both small and great, " stood to the covenant."

I have thus read my text, for the present and for six succeeding Discourses which it is my intention to address to you on the subject of. Confirmation. The light which it may contribute to that subject will appear as we proceed.

The distinct topics of my seven Discourses will be the following:

I. An Explanation of the Nature of the Rite of Confirmation.

This will be followed successively by six Addresses, viz.

II. To Parents, in reference to their Children whom they have devoted to God in Baptism.

III. To Sponsors,—" Godfathers and Godmothers."

* Gen. xvii. 12—14.

IV., V. To those persons who have not been confirmed, but who intend to present themselves to the
Bishop at a suitable time for that purpose.

VI. To the Congregation who have been confirmed, and are now by their own profession bound
by the covenant to which they have stood.

VII. To those who are now Candidates for Confirmation—after they shall have been confirmed, in view
of their participation of the Sacrament of the Lord's
Supper.

May the God of light and mercy vouchsafe his
grace and assistance to the feeble efforts of his Minister, enabling him faithfully to deliver his mind of the
truth, and blessing all of you by the instruction which
you may receive!

I am this morning to address you on *The Nature
of the Rite of Confirmation.* I make my appeal
calmly to your judgment. I ask only your unprejudiced and prayerful attention.

Before, however, I enter very intimately into the subject thus proposed to me, I must detain you on some
preliminary and, indeed, introductory observations.

In the first place, then, I observe, that it is the
primary purpose of the existence of a Church to promote, in obedience to the principles of Holy Scripture, the efficacy of those means through which the
Saviour has promised the communication of his grace*
—in prayer, for instance, in praise, in the public preach-
ing of the word, in the sacraments, and in all parts of

* Eph. iv. 11—16.

discipline for the edification of the body of Christ. In endeavouring to effect this, it is needful that the Church always, either in precept, where there is direct instruction, or in principle, where the rule is not literally prescribed, taking the Scripture for her guide, shall construct her services with a view of at once illustrating that which she would enforce, and, if possible, of securing and expressing the sincerity of those to whose edification she ministers. Thus all which is divinely appointed in the Sacrament of the Lord's Supper, (to pass, for the present, other of her services,) takes place in the solemn blessing of the elements, in the actual participation of the bread and wine, with the utterance, by the minister, of words in accordance with those made use of by the Lord when he first instituted that Sacrament;—all the rest of the service is affirmatory, under the discretion of the Church, of the faith and sincere devotion of those who minister and those who participate. In Confirmation, again, (to which subject I shall presently return,) the solemn rite is fulfilled in the prayer and blessing of the Bishop in the laying on of hands;—the rest of the service is affirmatory, under the discretion of the Church, of the faith and sincere devotion of those who minister and those who participate. In Baptism, the Sacrament is administered in the appointed use of water, "in the name of the Father, and of the Son, and of the Holy Ghost;"—all the rest of the service, I repeat it, is affirmatory, under the discretion of the Church, of the faith and the sincere devotion of those who minister and those who participate.

But, though this view of the subject takes away

from the immediately divine authority, not of the
Sacraments or the rites and ordinances, so far as
they are directly appointed of God, but of the services
with which they are accompanied and ministered, it
yet throws open before us, as members of that
Church, the field of self-examination; and if we are
persuaded, as well we may, (for inquiry on this point
is the paramount duty of every true Christian,) that
the Church has wisely used her discretion in constructing her services after the model of Scripture, it
then prescribes limits and offers aid to our humble
and prayerful efforts to discover the nature of those
blessings and those obligations which belong to us as
adopted children in the family of God.*

The connexion of these remarks with the subject
now before us will presently appear.

And, in reference to that subject, the first point to
which it applies is the mutual and inseparable dependance of the Sacrament of Baptism and the rite of Confirmation, which the Church understands and enforces. That dependance is so intimate, that it is impossible rightly to state the nature of Confirmation,
without having first unfolded to you the scriptural
doctrine of the Church on the nature of the Sacrament with which it is so connected. The time
demands of me that, on the present occasion, this
statement shall be as concise as possible.

The question so brought under our view, and on
which the whole mainly depends, may be expressed in
the following terms:

---

* 1 Cor. xiv. 26, 40, xi. 16; Heb. xiii. 7—9, and 17.

" *What position does Baptism hold in respect of that Regeneration or New Birth, without which no man can either see the kingdom of God in this world, or enter into its glory in another ?*"

Now, on this subject, as on very many others, the Scriptures speak, not doubtfully, indeed, but variously, and in such a manner that, by negligent, hasty, prejudiced, self-confident reading, we are likely to pervert them to error.

The following are conclusions to which they lead us. I beg only your calm attention. My object is to explain, not to explain away, the doctrine of the Church. Truth is wronged and our edification is impeded when we fear fixedly to contemplate that which claims to be Scripture verity, but which, for lack of adequate consideration, we take for granted to be erroneous.

The *essential* PART, then, of Regeneration, is that great moral change which passes on the human heart, by the influence and power of the Holy Spirit,* after the image of Christ. Of the commencement of this moral change, no man can accurately and definitely speak. Inward conviction—the order of Providence —the word of God—may in the hands of its Divine Author be the effecting instrument.† The Church affirms, (as we shall presently observe,) in more senses than one, that Baptism is *a* means whereby we receive the same, and a pledge to assure us thereof. Once commenced, it proceeds and increases through life;

---

* Ezek. xi. 19, 20; John iii. 6.
† 1 Pet. i. 23—25; John iii. 8.

and of the efficacy of the divinely-appointed means to this end, Baptism is a pledge to assure us. Thus far, however, we must here remark, that to this great moral *change of the heart* and of consequent character, all the *spiritual* blessings of the covenant are promised, in this world and the next.*

The *external* and visible PART of the New Birth is the rite of Baptism. By this we are, under the blessing of the Holy Spirit, introduced into and made members of the Church of Christ on earth, and so partakers of all those *external* privileges which that Church inherits in her militant state, and through which it is promised that the Holy Spirit shall promote the spiritual and eternal interests of the soul, and our discipline and edification to be the everlasting temple of God in heaven.† No man has a *covenant*‡ right to partake of these privileges of the Church until he has been made a member of that Church through the sacrament of Baptism. §

In the larger and stricter sense, then, Regeneration, or the New Birth, includes *both* of these PARTS—the change of the moral nature, and Baptism into the Church on earth.‖ For, although " with the heart man believeth unto righteousness, with the mouth confession is also made unto salvation."

But the Scriptures are not always careful to assert this connexion. They sometimes speak of the great

* Rom. ii. 25, 28, 29, viii. 1, 9, 14—17.

† Acts ii. 37—42, viii. 36—38; Heb. x. 22, 23; Eph. iv. 15, 16.

‡ Col. ii. 10—15.   § Mark xvi. 15, 16.

‖ Mark xvi. 16; Gal. iii. 26—29.

change which is the essential part of the New Birth, as itself the Regeneration to which all covenant blessings, for time and eternity, are attached. At other times, they affirm the same blessings in view of the outward sign which brings with it the means to the attainment of that end. And there are not wanting passages of Scripture in which the presence of both is either asserted or implied In the same Epistle of Peter, for instance, we read first that we are "born again, not of corruptible seed, but of incorruptible, by *the Word of God*, which liveth and abideth for ever;"* and then—after the figure of the ark which floated in safety on the waters—"*baptism* doth also now save us (not the putting away of the filth of the flesh, but the answer of a good conscience towards God) by the resurrection of Jesus Christ."† To which the Apostle Paul responds when he affirms, "Not by works of righteousness which we have done, but according to his mercy he saved us, by the *laver*, the bath, the font of regeneration, AND the renewing of the Holy Ghost."‡

From all that has been said, it would appear that in one view of this question, and that a limited one, the two points of the New Birth cannot be said ordinarily to have their *origin* at the same time.

Is the candidate for Baptism moved to approach the font by inward repentance and faith, which the Church requires?§ Then the great moral change has already taken its commencement. But does he,

---

* 1 Pet. i. 23.   † 1 Pet. iii. 21.
‡ Tit. iii. 5.   § See the Catechism.

impelled by whatever cause, approach self-deceived, or, as we shall presently observe, in *necessary* igno- rance? Then the right to the *external* privileges is accorded *before* the great moral change has taken place. In the former instance, there is a period during which, whatever may be the spiritual attain- ments of the candidate for admission into the Church on earth, the *covenant* claims to the privileges of that Church; and in the latter instance, whatever may be the promised efficacy of the means of grace, the claims to the *essential* and *spiritual privileges* of the Gospel, are equally *suspended*.

That the Church so interprets Scripture is manifest; for in reference to the *sincere* and enlightened partici- pators of Baptism, although, as we have seen, she requires of them the signs of the *previous* commence- ment of the great moral change, in repentance and faith—she plainly declares that the grace of the Sacra- ments is not the *first* movement of the Spirit of God in the heart, but that by the Sacraments, as means of spiritual good to us, peculiar and exclusive in their nature, "he doth work invisibly in us, and doth not only quicken, but also strengthen and confirm our faith in him;" that *same* faith, with a consistent re- pentance, having been already required of them who come to be baptized. But she so affirms the outward sign to be a *part* of the New Birth, by which we are introduced into the Church militant on earth, that, in a large but definite sense, though she requires in those who approach in sincerity and ask an interest in the blessings of the Church, that which is a manifesta- tion of the effectual *previous* commencement of the

spiritual life, she restricts her *definition* to the quick-
euing and confirming grace of the Sacraments, and
declares that the two parts of the New Birth being
now associated, herein and thus the baptized is rege-
nerated and born again—born of water and of the
Spirit. So much for those who at the time rightly
receive the Sacraments. With them, the period of
suspended blessings *precedes* the participation of
Baptism.

But the Church follows out this rule in reference to
infants, and to others, who are charitably received
into the number of God's people on their perhaps
ignorant profession of a right faith. The proper sign,
on the part of God, of the Church, and of the member
of the Church, of the right of the baptized to all the
blessings conveyed by promise to God's people, is the
permission to partake of the Sacrament of the Lord's
Supper, and therein to approach the footstool of the
throne of grace as one accepted and fully blessed in
Christ Jesus.

Now that privilege the administration of Baptism
does not necessarily convey. Time is given for subsequent self-examination, for the instruction of the
Church, the use of the means granted to the baptized,
and the examination of appointed ministers, followed
by the Confirmation of the Bishop, before the full
membership of the baptized is ratified. In the case,
then, of those who are baptized in necessary ignorance, as of infants, or of those whose *profession* of
faith and repentance is charitably received, the *sus-
pension* of privilege takes place *after* the reception
of the outward sign, and that privilege is ratified in

the rite of Confirmation. Though Baptism is in "the laver of Regeneration," the renewing of the Holy Ghost takes a far wider range, and *includes* in its course the grace of Baptism as the *distinctive* and CONNECTING element of the New Birth.

And now, to make these matters yet the more clear, let us occupy a few moments in contrasting with what has been said, and with each other, the prevailing errors of the present day. They lie, as for the most part all errors lie, in extremes.

There are those, for instance, who think that Regeneration is so exclusively in that which is the essential part of it—the great moral change of the heart—that the outward rite is, at the most, only figurative, and may therefore be, without danger, altogether set aside. They live and they die unbaptized.*

Others, and they are many, very intimately symbolize with these. They dare not resist the plain intimations of Scripture, that the Sacraments are "generally necessary to salvation;" but then, as though in this one instance a *legal ceremony* had been reserved to the Church, they satisfy themselves in the misbelief that those Sacraments are not in a peculiar sense a means of grace, but only an outward figure or type, which is to produce a sort of natural movement in the affections; that they are "merely badges and tokens of Christian men's profession," and not, by God's mercy, "*effectual* signs of grace."

The Romish Church, on the other hand, with those who symbolize or draw near to symbolize with her,—

---

* 2 Kings v. 8—14; Matt. iii. 13—17.

and, sooth to say, at the present time we are even in danger of this,—the Romish Church, so far from restricting Regeneration to the moral change of the heart, attributes all to the ministration of the external sign, by the hands of those who are appointed to baptize, and holds it forth to be believed, that, without regard to the state of him who seeks Baptism, or even of him who ministers it, the grace is communicated, as from a deposit of grace entrusted to the Church, to whomsoever it may be who partakes of the Sacrament; and that, strange to say, Baptism, as such, brings with it remission of original sin, justification, sanctification and eternal life.

Amidst all these conflicting errors, the Church of England takes a safe and middle course.

She never administers Baptism—the Sacrament of the New Birth—without, in the case of them of riper years, the presumption of the spiritual life in those who are to be partakers of it; and then she regards the UNITING grace of both the sign and the spiritual sanctification of the heart, as the grace of Regeneration.

The case of infants offers a necessary exception. They who doubt whether God enters into covenant with man in his extremest infancy, may obtain satisfaction by reading the seventeenth chapter of the book of Genesis. The Church has from the first held it to be according to the mind of God in the Scriptures, that Baptism should be administered to infants.* Does she, then, believe that in the case of infants

* Acts ii. 38, 39; Mark ix. 13—16.

grace accompanies the administration? So far as the necessity of the case will allow, she does. For repentance and faith, in the nature of things she cannot look; the signs, that is, of *antecedent* spiritual life, she cannot expect. But these things she does look for in the parents and sponsors. She brings to her aid earnest and fervent prayer, which God has pledged himself to hear and to answer. She claims a solemn promise, that from the first movement of feeling and intelligence, the child shall be carefully trained up to the service of God; and then—can she doubt it?—she believes that the Spirit of God is present, attesting in that Sacrament the truth of God's promises, and sanctioning the delegated authority of the Church to admit even an infant into the number of her members, to hold a covenant right to *the use of all those* means of grace to which God has *promised* his spiritual blessing.

In the case of adults, the New Birth into the outward Church in view of all her privileges, is perfected by Baptism AFTER the commencement of the great moral change which is wrought in the heart by the operation of the Holy Ghost.

In the case of infancy, the New Birth by Baptism into the Church, in respect of her formal but effectual privileges, may accompany, it may precede, the great moral change; and so that great moral change take place AFTER the admission of the baptized into the Church, in view of a participation of her external but effectual privileges. Until that change has commenced, the *spiritual* and *eternal* blessings of the covenant are *suspended*, and the baptized has, therefore, no right granted to him to partake of the other Sacrament—the pledge, as that Sacrament is, of his personal interest in the higher and ultimate blessings of the covenant.

In this middle course the Church of England holds her way; avoiding the errors of both extremes— regardless of metaphysical niceties—desirous alone of being scriptural, and successful in her attempt.

We are now prepared to enter on our statement of the nature of the rite of Confirmation, and, after our introductory remarks, little time need be occupied in making that statement.

No person who carefully reads in the New Testament the history of the early Church, can reasonably doubt that the labours of the subordinate ministers were under the revisal of the higher officers of the Christian community—that the apostles visited the several churches to examine into the effect of the ministry of the word, and, as it is there expressed, with what exact intention I do not now pause to inquire, to *confirm* the churches. It is as little to be doubted that, in conveying the blessing of the high office which they held, they laid their hands on the converts whom they so acknowledged and received. And it is equally manifest that God mercifully concurred in the Confirmation so administered.* Now, without offering any speculation on the nature of the Confirmation to which reference is made in these passages, the Church, we may observe, in the use of her discretion, imitates, as far as the case will allow, the

* Acts xiv. 21—23, xv. 41, viii. 14—17; Heb. vi. 2.

apostolic practice. The baptized and instructed are presented to the Bishop, who, on being assured of their faithfulness and sincerity, confirms to them the blessings of the covenant to which they have surrendered themselves.

Where the candidates have been baptized in their riper years, then, in Confirmation, on the declaration of those who present themselves, that they hold to the profession which they made at their Baptism, the act of the subordinte minister is acknowledged, and the full admission of the baptized into the privileges of the Church is confirmed by the highest officer—the Bishop. Nor does the Church doubt, that as the extraordinary gifts of the Spirit were conveyed by the laying on of the hands of the apostles, so, in this instance, the Holy Ghost is present, and, with measured blessing, sanctions the work of his appointed servant.

Where Baptism has taken place in infancy, though the mode and issue of Confirmation is the same, yet the conditions are somewhat changed—they partake of that character which *the necessity of the case* requires. Here the use of the means of grace, instruction, knowledge, faith, obedience, have all taken place, *within the promises*, indeed, but AFTER Baptism, by which those promises, so far as they regarded *the means* of salvation, were visibly signed and sealed.

What, then, is the actual state of a young person, who has been baptized in infancy, before and in respect of Confirmation?

I will illustrate it by a supposed, but possible case.

It had been possible that an estate should have been given to him in his infancy, to the actual possession of which certain conditions were attached, which he must himself thereafter recognize and attest—it might have been now given to him on a covenant, to the terms of which his parents or other representatives were required, for the present, to affix their signatures— solemnly engaging thereby, with the aid afforded to them by the returns of that estate, carefully and earnestly to administer an education suitable to the expectations so created. The personal possession or the ultimate loss of the benefit intended would, in such a case, depend on the result of the education so administered—the personal concurrence, that is, of the infant, when at an age to determine and act for himself, in the terms to which his representatives had pledged their sincerity. In this case, would there not be, as it were, a renewal, even to a constructive re-originating of the covenant—its obligations and its blessings—when the signature was so affixed? The mind of him who bestowed the gift itself would not, indeed, be changed. The gift itself could scarcely be said to be enlarged. The benefactor has throughout surely kept and performed his part of the covenant; but the full appropriation has been, by necessity of the, as yet, imperfect intentions and will of the infant respecting it, to the present moment suspended.

In such a supposed case, we have an illustration of the state of one baptized in infancy, in respect of Confirmation. The blessings of the covenant were conditionally but, in the means, actually given to him at his Baptism—given, in fact, not to himself individually, who, of the necessity of the case, was incapable of appreciating and using them, but to his parents and representatives, for his good—to be expended in his instruction and discipline for everlasting life; and, when he arrived at a suitable age and adequate religious attainments to be claimed by himself and confirmed to him on his own sincere profession of faith and obedience.

These things being premised, respecting the state of those who have been baptized in infancy, the nature of Confirmation is in all cases the same. The person presenting himself to be confirmed, declares before the Church, that *he stands to the covenant.* The Bishop acknowledges the declaration, renews to him the promises of God's grace and favour, and, by the highest earthly authority in such a case, admits him to the full participation of the blessings which God has given to his Church on earth, in anticipation of and preparation for her glory in another world.

Much is still left to be observed on this subject. A wide field of instruction is thrown open before me. On the next Sunday morning I shall address those of you who are parents, and who have devoted children to God in Baptism, in view of their subsequent Confirmation.

SERMON II.

THE OBLIGATIONS AND THE HOPES

OF

PARENTS

IN RESPECT OF THEIR CHILDREN BAPTIZED IN
INFANCY.

----

2 KINGS xxiii. 3:

And all the people stood to the covenant.

THE arrangement I proposed of subjects for my
Lectures on Confirmation, leads me this morning to
address those of you who are parents, and who have
devoted your children to God in Baptism, in view of
their being hereafter presented to the Bishop to be
confirmed.

The subject is in a high sense exclusive, and in
some part fraught with difficulties; not because it is
in itself wanting in simplicity, but because it lies so
near to every man's convictions, and so forces itself
on every man's thoughts, that there are few who do
not come at last to imagine that their own opinion

respecting it is truth, and, in consequence, to give
slight attention to the argument which ought to dispose them to suspect that they may somehow have
mistaken first principles, and be pursuing their course
in fatal, though not irremediable error.

We have before us, then, the following twofold
question : *" What are the* OBLIGATIONS *and* THE HOPES
of parents in respect of their children, YET IN IN-
FANCY, *who by their choice and concurrence were,
shortly after their birth, baptized into the Church of
Christ?"*

On this subject, without distinctly again referring to
the division so suggested, I shall arrange the thoughts
which I have to offer to you under the three following
heads :—the *obligations* of Christian parents in respect
of their baptized children—the *range of their duties,*
and—the *proper limits* of their *hopes;* that is, in
other words, my discourse will contemplate severally
YOURSELVES, your CHILDREN and the COVENANT.

For, I presume, as, indeed, I have already hinted,
that, although the Church does not, for reasons to
which I shall have occasion to refer in my next Lec-
ture, recognize the parents, as such, in the order of her
baptismal service, yet you heartily concurred in your
child's Baptism ; that, being yourselves Christians
you did so from conviction, after much meditation
and prayer; and, moreover, that, knowing as you did,
that Baptism itself takes place in the use of the few
words and the very simple administration which our
Lord himself instituted, your concurrence included,
freely on your part, all the doctrine of the Church,
and the large views of obligation and blessing which

her form of Baptismal Service implies. You were yourselves, it may be, present, and so personally and devoutly gave your sanction to all this; and, in a sense to which I shall again refer, as it were, renewed your own acquiescence in all the terms of the covenant, in the Baptism of your child.

What, then, is the distinctive outline of the relationship thus unfolded to our view? We have here a parent, not (most unreasonable and unchristian presumption!) deferring the use of the effectual sign and pledge of the covenant, until the intellect and, in some sense, the passions shall have attained their maturity, but knowingly and purposely bringing to the " laver" a *very infant*, in a state necessarily and utterly incapable of any conception of the part which he is fulfilling—of either assent or disapproval; laying that infant under obligations which have respect to the eye of the all-wise God; and claiming for it, on the terms of a covenant, conditional blessings which contemplate his whole existence, both in the present world and in the next.

Now, with such a statement before us, what must be the original reflections suggested to us?

The Scriptures contemplate the whole range of human life—all its capabilities, all its dangers, its present and its future hopes and fears, with the intimate connexion of all these with the several relationships which attend us and influence our movements and our habits, in our immediate state; and in this large view they affectingly make their appeal—" Can a woman forget her sucking child, that she should not have compassion on the son of her womb?" May we not add, Can a father, possessing a knowledge of the terms of the highest human happiness, and affirming his own supreme and earnest desire to be interested in those terms, neglect to use the power which is granted to him to bring his child within the range of the blessings so offered to him? Can Christian parents willingly fail to "train up a child in the way in which he should go," in order to the attainment of the favour of God in the present world, and his eternal glory in the next?

But you have already acknowledged this your obligation—this covenant obligation of your nature and the existence of your offspring—and, in effect, you have professed, before the Church, your firm but dependant determination to fulfil it. Had you been Heathen parents, you might have been imagined ignorantly to surrender your child to the pledged education of his sponsors; but you are Christian and enlightened parents. You gave your child willingly and intelligently to the terms of the Christian covenant. You have learned to discriminate between your own duties and those of the sponsors. You never intended to surrender the EDUCATION of your child to them; but your concurrence fully implied, that whatever depended on you for the preparation of your infant for the high destiny which was before him, you would yourselves give. The Church received your child as devoted to the Lord. The child was again placed in your arms and restored to your home, that you might fulfil your pledge, and do all which a parent might do to promote its everlasting welfare. But that performance, so far as you are concerned—

and how far, too, for the child also!—involved the security of those blessings which, in presenting him for Baptism, you seemed to demand for your infant.

Can any thing be imagined more consistent with all we are taught to believe respecting God, the grace of the Gospel and the economy of his Church, than the combination thus brought before us?—A covenant for the salvation of a responsible being in infancy—wherein, for the present and eternal welfare of the child, God promising the gift of his Spirit, the Church, the parents, the sponsors, are all made interested parties, and, (the appropriation of those blessings left still suspended,) the pledge is given on all hands to minister such a holy training and discipline, that, the Holy Spirit graciously blessing human endeavours, the infant, as years proceed and nature asserts her maturer powers, may learn to refuse the evil and choose the good, and so devote himself to the service of the Most High, that he may claim the gracious boon.

Taking a lower view of human existence, I ask, in illustration of what has been said, Has not many a parent, holding his infant in his arms, anticipated with confidence, in the education he intended to administer, his future station and destiny in the present life? Had that parent *held consistently* to his confidence, and had *adequate assistance* been given to him from above, the result would have certainly followed, and his hopes and purposes certainly been fulfilled.

But here another question demands our careful notice.

If an infant may be the subject of a covenant before
he is capable of estimating either the obligations which
are thereby bound upon him, or the blessings which
are so conferred, and that, all dependant on the result
of education to which God has promised his concurrence and blessing—at what moment must that education *commence?* When may a child be said to be
first capable of *religious* education?

Now I will not hesitate to assert, in the first instance, what I will immediately proceed to illustrate,
that an infant is received into covenant by Baptism,
because from the moment of his Baptism, were that
Baptism administered as early as the covenant seal
was granted to the Church of Israel,—from the
moment of his Baptism, he is not only capable of, but
necessarily subject to an education which affects his
religious character and hopes. Religious influences
begin with the birth—they become *conditions of the
covenant* of salvation at Baptism.

Let us see how this applies.

We were born, all, children of wrath—that is, with
propensities of mind easily developed and formed to
sin by those incitements to evil by which we are sur-
rounded, and which have vitality and direction given
to them by the Prince of the Power of the Air—but
which may also be subdued to the renewal of the
heart by holy influences, blessed and quickened by
the Holy Spirit of God.

They who have treated of the training of the young
in the way in which they should go, have taught us,
for the most part, to arrange the subject under two
heads—those of instruction and education—the latter

implying all proper modes of unfolding and giving vigour to the mental and bodily powers; and the former, the communication of knowledge, whether religious or other, for its various purposes. And they add, generally, that the desired end is to be promoted through *learning, discipline* and *example.* Now all this is very true, if applied at the right time and after the right mode,—these are parts of a truly religious training, if they are administered on religious principles and for truly religious ends; but they do not reach the subject before us,—they do not contemplate, that is, the very infancy of human life,—they begin not with the obligations of the covenant. Education, to be effectual of its ends, must adapt itself to the actual state, powers, or want of power, of the educated. An infant is incapable of the forms of truth; its movements of thought and of observation are, in the first instance, if they may be said to exist at all, of the very feeblest texture. And yet is an infant capable of the strongest impressions, and all the movements of its being are subject to influences from without.

Is this true? Observe then the consequences which follow upon it.

The foundations of all character are in morals—that is, in the first instance, in the dispositions of the heart; and those dispositions are not in themselves reason-able, though they become eventually subject to a mind governed by reason; but meantime, *before* reason can be said to have *any* direction, and therefore long before it is cultivated to the exercise of its powers, the heart may be influenced and subdued. In truth, the whole question now before us, is involved in the use of another instrument in the right training of the young. *Before* discipline or example or instruction, and more largely, for the ends we have in view, *throughout* the progress of all these, is SYMPATHY.

A very infant (baptized whenever he may be) *sympathizes* with parental love and parental authority, before he is able to discriminate and assent to either the one or the other; and therein is the commencement, and, for a time, the whole substance, of religious education. I may illustrate this by an appeal to any affectionate mother before me, on the marked influence of soothing sounds, or of sharp and irritating intonations, whether addressed directly to the child or otherwise, on the very nature of infancy—and I may ask such, if they have not observed how progressively these infant emotions have combined themselves with the opening faculties of attention, contemplation, definite desire, the acquirement of knowledge, and the rest?

The religious education, then, of an *infant* is in the *right regulation of the sympathies*, and, for this, in the direct and marked and expressed, always expressed, dominion of religious affections — those affections, without reason, in *the first instance*, and subsequently, but orderly, combining themselves with all the enlarging means of discipline and instruction.

And all this is as, in the FIRST INSTANCE, but *the preparing of the soil* for the future seed of truth, not one grain of which has yet been dropped into it; and SUBSEQUENTLY, the loosening, the weeding and watering of that soil, that the growth of that which has been judiciously committed to the bosom of the earth may be the more healthful and productive. Religion is Truth germinating, striking, growing and made fruitful in the sympathies of the heart, and thence in the conduct of the whole life.

And now, however diversified may be the *instruments* of the education of the young, and they are necessarily many, have we not clearly discovered the appropriate place of that part which is administered by the parent? Knowledge and some sort of discipline, a child must gradually obtain from every hand; but all this, and from the very commencement of life and the first opening of the faculties, in due subservience to the higher and proper ends of a religious life, wisely regulated by *paternal authority*, and affectionately mingled with the *love* of a *mother's heart*,—all this, for the purposes of the covenant, he must receive from his parents alone!

And here I touch upon a subject which has been before my mind throughout my discourse. Has it not throughout been implied that parents, in order to fulfil their covenant duties to those whom God has entrusted to their care, must themselves be, in the highest and proper sense, religious?—that their religion must sink deep into their affections, and as deeply move and regulate the *sympathies* of their hearts? It is not enough that they approve what is right, or even communicate and enforce it. It is not enough, in this primary view, (for how can an infant observe it?) that, as a question of example, their lives be, even to the utmost limit of self-denial and obedience to the known will of God, surrendered to the obligations of religion.

They must *feel* what is holy, and give due and consistent *expression* to it.   The love of God in their souls
must contemplate the manifestations of the Divine
compassion to their child as well as to themselves;
their desire of salvation must involve his eternal welfare; their faith and diligence and hope must include
within their range all which is connected with the spiritual well-being of their infant.   The religion of a
parent, in fact, *embraces*—includes within itself, also
the religion of the child; and, in a very important
sense, the parent cultivates the manifestations of the
grace of God in his offspring by cultivating them in
himself.

There is this, moreover, attendant on what has thus
been stated.   The *early* movements of a life devoted
to God are like the tender shoots first springing forth
from the earth, which need the watchful care and
cultivation of the husbandman, but reward his continued and persevering anxiety by the vigour and
fruitfulness of their growth.   When religion first com-
municates of its holy influence to the mind *after* the
natural powers are matured, how frequently do we
see its progress and growth in perverted forms—the
fruit is hardly brought to perfection.   But when it
has been administered while the sympathies alone
were awake, the knowledge, faith, holiness, experience of the parent accompany the progressive increase
of all which is holy in the child, until habits are
formed and every pledge is given of a self-denying,
sober and persevering consistency throughout the
religious life.

But our remarks must here assume a different form. Whatsoever may be the *apparent* connexion between a rightly-administered education and good results, that connexion is by no means *original* and *certain*. The nature of a *plant*, indeed, will perhaps necessarily obey the hand of the cultivator; but man is born in sin, and his tendency is from the womb to go astray;—religion finds not in his bosom a native soil or a favouring atmosphere. Whence, then, do the fond hopes of a religious parent derive their firmness and stability? Do you say they must rely on the grace of God, and submit silently to his manifested will? How frequently are great truths uttered, which become erroneous by the mode in which we receive them! A negligent and unconditional reliance on the grace of God, or that which regards that grace as so distributed as to leave the Most High unfaithful to his promises, are unjustified equally by Scripture and by fact.

Let my text rather supply the answer. The grace of God flows from the fountain of the Divine Mind through the channels or means by which he has said that he will communicate it. When God first gave that law to which my text refers, he declared his mind respecting it—"I make a covenant."* Does our heart, with the people of Israel, respond to the affirmation of the Most High? Do we on our part say, "I stand to the covenant!" Then the blessings,—the grace of that covenant are ours. Our hopes rest safely on what God has promised to communicate to

---

* Exodus xxxiv. 10.

those who are, according to the covenant, obedient to his will.

How, then, does this apply to the question now before us?

To us the words of the covenant are all the words of the Bible—the law perfectly developed, fulfilled and illustrated. Do you ask me then, what good hope you have that your efforts to train up your child in the way in which he should go, will be effectual of the desired end? I answer, asking again, Do you stand to the covenant? And to obtain a safe answer to this last question, let us return to what has been already suggested respecting education, and trace its connexion onward through life.

Must you be yourself truly religious in order to communicate, not religious knowledge alone, but, which is equally and *primarily* necessary also, *religious influences* to your child? Your religion must *personally* be THE RELIGION OF THE COVENANT, or it is not within the sphere of the blessing; it must be the religion, that is, of the Bible. Fall short of this, and on what do your hopes rest? You have no assurance of God's blessing and grace but in Christ Jesus. Worldly parents will probably train up their children to various measures of worldliness. A merely moral parent will educate for morality. He who, from whatever cause, holds partial or erroneous views of the truths and obligations of Scripture, will impress on the mind and character of his offspring all the uncertainty, or all the self-will and obstinacy, of error.

These are *natural* results, without the blessing of God. And where even truth prevails, that which is inconsistent in practice, from a like cause must produce similar results. You may appeal to the actual state of society for a proof of all which is here asserted. You may there fix your thoughts on the varied forms of human character, and easily trace, in each case, results to their causes. In how many instances cross lights of truth, admitted partially and suspiciously, have made only "darkness visible"! In how many more, (the terms of the economy of our salvation having been administered negligently and subordinately,— that is, having been made doubtful and dishonoured,) men have attained to the maturity of intellectual power and acquirement before they have escaped from the very infancy of religious knowledge and character! He alone who stands to the covenant, in all its requirements and in view of all its promises, has a just right to hope for the attendant grace of God—and *that hope will never be disappointed.* But how seldom is this the actual state of things! How generally do even religious parents feel themselves driven back, as it were, by their own inconsistencies and errors, to a reliance on the grace of God alone, almost irrespectively of the covenant of grace!

But the subject is larger yet. If we must ourselves be obedient members of the covenant, fully to justify an expectation of the blessings promised in the covenant for our children, we must also *minister their education after the same rule.* To train up a child in the way in which he should go, is to train him up in the way of the covenant; that is, in plain words, in the way of the Bible. If you wish all the promises made to your child in Baptism to be fulfilled, you must from the first dawn of his intellectual and moral nature, and until he is of age to take these things on himself, instruct and educate him in simple accordance with the Scriptures. All the ordinary motives which prevail among men in respect of the training of the young, must at best be secondary, in your view, to those which you find there ; and if opposed in any measure to the right and large influence of the truth as it is in Jesus, they must be cordially and wholly deprecated and renounced.

You must take for granted all which the Scriptures —the words of the covenant—say respecting the actual, the fallen, the corrupt, the naturally lost state of your infant, and bear in mind that in education you are not merely unfolding that which has a tendency to good, but that you have yet more to do in correcting and restraining to a contrary and opposing habit that which is essentially evil.

The standard of righteousness to which you propose to raise your child, must be that of the Word of God, comprising all its various parts—repentance for sin, faith in Christ, conversion, obedience to the known will of the Most High, self-control, consistency, per-. severance.

You must endeavour, as soon as possible, to find a place in the heart of your child for those motives which the covenant affords and to which it appeals. To regulate his conduct by the desire of present good or reputation, or even of affording pleasure to you, are at the best but secondary motives. Let them, as soon as possible, be made second to those which arise from a contemplation of the grace, the love, the glory of the cross. How numberless are the motives to obedience to the covenant which are afforded by the Gospel! From these, as a wise master-builder, the parent must choose, adapting them to the rising, the ever-varying exigencies of the case—these, from the first desire of the pardon of sin, to the fear which is as darkness, and the hope which is full of immortality.

Then must you bear in mind that (to warn and to encourage you) the Scriptures bring before us instances of success and of failure in the education of the young.

Like Hannah, give your child to God, and train him to his high destinies *from his birth*—the holiness of a Samuel may be the result.

Like Abraham, *command* your children and your household after you, that they keep the way of the Lord to do judgment and justice—and the blessings of the covenant shall rest upon them.

But be *unlike* Lot, who relied on the natural force of religious education, and took his children into the world, where they perished with the wicked.

Be *unlike* Aaron, who set his children an example of idolatry, and his first-born perished in their impiety.

Be *unlike* Eli, whose weak affections put not adequate restraints on the evil tendencies of his sons— and he lived just long enough to see and repent under the fearful punishment which came upon them.

Is there, then, in truth a reasonable and sure hope in obedience to the terms of the covenant? Happily, the promises are not only given in general terms to those who are in Christ Jesus, but they attach themselves to those means through which the grace of God is conveyed to us.

To the reading and the hearing of the Word of God, the blessing of faith and of obedience is attached. Let it, then, be one of your first objects to make your child acquainted with the Scriptures, and dispose him to read for the promised ends.

To the observation of the Sabbath peculiar grace is given. Place your child in circumstances, and largely form such habits in him, as may assure to him this result.

He who asks, we read, shall be heard and answered in Christ Jesus. Instruct your child in the holy art of prayer. Pray with him. Let prayer be a household custom. Lead him onward to the personal habit of prayer, as you would teach him the first movements of his person or his tongue.

All the economy of the Church, too, is arranged to make effectual the blessings of the covenant. Far, far from efforts to educate, be controversial forms of religious truth; but education to holiness, including edification in union with the body of Christ, must connect itself with the ordinances of the Church. How large is this subject, and how neglected! And yet is there therein something intimately connected with that which is more immediately before us. The Church is the mother of us all. Her very existence in the favour of God depends upon her faithful minis-trations to the spiritual and eternal welfare of his children, and that in modes best calculated to pro-mote true religion in all periods of the life. The

wise parent will trace the connexion of his best hopes
with obedience to her institutions. He will train up
his child with a view of his entering seriously and
affectionately into her services, that he may partake,
now and for ever, of the blessings which God has
granted to her in her Saviour.

But, after all, as the grace of God connects the
means of our spiritual welfare with their results, so
prayer, of God's mercy and through the intercession
of our ascended Lord, seeks and secures to us that
grace. All our endeavours must be in vain without
the persevering exercise of this duty. None can be
in vain if, being according to the covenant, they be
forwarded by that grace which will assuredly be
accorded to us in answer to our earnest, persevering
and faithful prayers.

Am I asked, then, wherein lie the obligations and
the hopes of truly Christian parents, in respect of
their children whom they have already presented at
the font for Baptism, and intend soon to present to
the Bishop to be confirmed? I answer, Like the
Israelites, with the volume of inspiration open before
them they have in their own name and for their
children, "made a covenant before the Lord, to walk
after the Lord, and to keep his commandments and
his testimonies and his statutes, with all their heart
and all their soul, to perform the words of the covenant which are written in that book!" Like the Israelites, then, let them "stand to the covenant"!

SERMON III.

THE DUTIES OF SPONSORS.

2 KINGS xxiii. 3:

And all the people stood to the covenant.

I HAVE been studiously careful thus far, in my
Lectures on Confirmation, to note the distinction
which exists between that which is of Divine appoint-
ment and authority in a religious rite or sacrament,
and that which the Church has judged expedient to
add thereto; the one being absolutely necessary to
the existence of the rite or sacrament, and the rest
necessary to those alone who have bound themselves
to the prescribed mode of the observance of it. For
instance, addressing his eleven disciples in Galilee,
our Lord thus renewed the institution of the Sacrament of Baptism: *Go, ye, and teach all nations, bap-*
tizing them in the name of the Father, and of the
Son, and of the Holy Ghost. All, then, which is of
Divine authority in the Sacrament of Baptism, takes
place when he who may rightly undertake that office
either immerses or sprinkles with water, as the case
may be, one adequately taught, " in the name of the

Father, and of the Son, and of the Holy Ghost." All the rest of the service is added by the Church.

But although we may thus have reached the limits of Divine authority, and may therefore truly say that he who is not thus far baptized is not a Christian, we have not reached the proper limits of obligation—obligation which may not be safely transgressed by him who claims the hopes of the covenant. The Apostle Paul more than once expresses himself in the following manner, and, in this instance, in reference expressly to the Sacrament of the Lord's Supper:*
"All things are lawful for me, but all things are not *expedient;* all things are lawful for me, but all things *edify* not." Beyond, then, the direct and prescribed authority of Divine law, *expediency* and *edification*, when once discovered, afford rules to guide the heart and the conduct of enlightened Christians.

But this assertion, though thus far apostolic, needs much guarding in its application.

In proportion as we claim for ourselves to be judges of what is expedient and for edification, must we be cautious, humble, prayerful—not laying as a burden upon others that in which we think we have discovered a safe rule for our own thoughts and conduct.

But, on the other hand, *the Church*, under conditions which I will presently suggest, may safely enjoin upon her *members* that which *she* believes to be expedient to the edifying of the body of Christ.

These things, however, she may do—never without Scripture—always in strict accordance with principles plainly deducible from the Word of God—and, where

* 1 Cor. x. 23.

it is possible, taking her initiative from some element of the proposed service or institution, which is of confessed Divine origin, and to which she can therein plainly and throughout refer.

That which the Church urges as expedient, that is, must be of the nature of the development of a known and acknowledged Divine law, and thus far gather to itself authority from that law!

Now if this rule prevail, the Church must always indeed retain her institutions under correction of the farther light of that to which she traces them as to a source. But, on the question of the force of what is so said to be expedient and for edification, if it be possible by an appeal to the whole history of the Church of the Saviour, especially in its earliest and least corrupted periods, assisted by the Word of God, to discover wherein she has throughout enforced that which is according to the mind of the Most High, would it not argue, to say the least, a most unsafe religious state, whatever might be the *private* sentiments of an individual respecting that expediency, (for opinions vary with the progress of knowledge,) so to *oppose* those sentiments to the judgment and experience of the Church on these matters as to promote divisions? Doubts in individuals may stimulate inquiry, but they must not be followed out to the creation of schism.

The principles which have guided the Church in the purest periods of her history, in obedience to what she has deemed expedient for the edification of her members, when constructing her religious services, it is by no means difficult to trace.

She has kept ever in view, on the one hand, the changeless faithfulness of God, and, on the other, the sinfulness of man. She has looked upon the promises of the Divine Word as in themselves infallible, but she has at the same time contemplated the infirmity of human beings, to whom those promises are addressed, as rendering them, so far as man can judge, of uncertain personal application. She has never doubted the efficacy of the means of grace through which the promises are made sure to us, but she has not hid from her eyes that he who uses these means may be in a state of mind unprepared to be a recipient of that grace.

With all these things before her, the Church has constructed her services in such a manner as to seem to involve contradictions. She dare not hesitate to affirm the certain fulfilment, on his part, of all which God has promised. But on the part of the recipient of his grace, she has proceeded with the utmost care and circumspection.

The service for the Baptism of Infants is a large illustration of all that has been thus affirmed.

In that service it is manifest the Church believes that Baptism is the means appointed by God for introducing the recipient into the number of his people on earth, in order to farther instruction and grace to everlasting life. To the baptized, the promises of God given to the Church begin, immediately on their introduction into the Church, to be effectual, through the Spirit, *on the conditions on which* those promises are held forth.

She illustrates her view of this principle, and therein of the faithfulness of God to his promise to receive all who come to him, by reference to an act of the

Saviour, in itself disconnected from Baptism. He took into his arms and blessed infants presented to him by their parents or friends, and rebuked those who forbad them.

And because she regards no promise of the new covenant as isolated from the rest, she farther affirms the truth of God by the use of other means on which he has said that results shall follow, including that which she anticipates through the Sacrament. She reminds the people, that if God blesses the Sacraments, he hears prayer also, and therefore guides them in asking for the Holy Spirit, that the greatest of all gifts may be bestowed on the baptized.*

Then, on the other part, knowing as she does that the promises, though in themselves true, are yet, in respect of individuals, conditional, and that although God knows the heart and may pronounce the blessing without reserve, man—the Church—does not know the heart, and must therefore *presume* alone the existence of that which assures the effect of the means;—in her great caution, where affirmation of a prepared and holy state can be affirmed before witnesses, as in the case of adults, she demands both the witnesses and the affirmation; but where, as in infants, that state cannot be affirmed, knowing, from the testimony of Scripture, that God does nevertheless enter into covenant with infants, and calling in the aid of the promises given, not to education as a whole, but in particular to all those means which must be daily and hourly used in order to such an education, she appoints sponsors—

---

* Comp. Matt. vii. 7, and Luke xi. 9—13.

godfathers and godmothers—who, in faith of God's promises, and in sincere purpose to make faithful use of the means to the desired and promised end, at once pledge themselves for the child, and offer themselves in all their efforts and prayers as channels, if I may so express myself, through which the grace of God may flow to the infant.

You hesitate to receive this. Your mind reverts to facts. You look around you and ask, Where are the manifestations of these things?

I speak not, for the present, of things as they are, but as they ought to be. I am not describing the actual state of the Church, but the principle which pervades her institutions and her services. *The Church errs not* IN DOCTRINE, *but she fails* IN DISCIPLINE. Well were it for true religion, if, instead of satisfying themselves with endeavouring to find out what they suppose to be the mistakes in principle of the Church, men would strenuously and personally endeavour to give force and efficacy to her institutions for effecting the purposes of grace amongst them!

And now, what would be the state of the case if the discipline of the Church were followed out in respect of the sponsors of baptized infants?

Have you never reflected on the very peculiar position which a sponsor is supposed to hold when presenting a child at the font for Baptism? He makes his responses in his own person, and yet he would seem in those responses also to personate or be the representative of the child. Now there is only one mode in which we can explain or justify this assumption of the Church, and that is in a presumed full and unreserved belief of the promises of God, conjoined with a deep and consistent sincerity of heart and conduct in him who fills the responsible office.   Let the sponsor only believe that God will fulfil his promises, hear prayer, and bless the means of education from the Baptism of the infant; let him sincerely and humbly intend to make use of those means from the moment when the child shall have been received into the Church—then all is in its place and order in the service; the sponsor may speak for himself and for the child—he may anticipate the blessing, and be prepared to receive that blessing on the part of the child, and from that time forward minister it to him for his present and his eternal good.   He may believe, as the Church teaches, that *now*, (for in respect of the infant this is the first act of COVENANT EDUCATION,) *now* God hears, *now* God answers, *now* God gives his Holy Spirit, *now* God receives the infant into the number of his children— inheritors of the privileges of the kingdom of heaven in this world, in view of the great issue in the next.

As has, then, been already affirmed respecting parents who have devoted their children to God in Baptism, so now, with the services and institutions of the Church before us, must the like be affirmed of sponsors.

Godfathers and godmothers must, in the view of the Church, *be holy persons.* They must person- ally and practically and perseveringly respond to all the terms of the covenant.   They must, the Church elsewhere affirms, as a formal affirmation of all these things, be participators of the Sacrament of the Lord's Supper.   They must truly believe all the promises of God's Word which bear (and they all bear) upon the commencement and the progress of the discipline and education of the human mind. They must be willing to involve their own spiritual and eternal interests in those of the child whom they represent. They must intend, seriously, to do all which lies in their power to promote the truly religious education of the infant until the mind be formed to respond according to the answers which they have given, on his behalf, in the solemn service of his admission into the Church; and they must be ready now to commence, in the full assurance that, God inspiring and aiding their sincerity, *the effort shall not be in vain.*

The discretion of the Church in appointing this office for the edification of the body of Christ, may be made yet more manifest.

It would appear that, in the earliest ages, the sponsors of infants were, for the most part, though not exclusively, the *parents* themselves.* They pledged themselves, in the face of God and the congregation of his people, to bring up the child, which they now presented at the font, in the nurture and admonition of the Lord. Their promise was accepted, and the child thereupon enrolled amongst the members of the Church.

Days of persecution, however, and the case of the parentless infants, left, from whatever cause, in the hands of Christians, rendered this mode of security for the holy discipline of the opening mind uncertain. The caution of the Church was awakened, and soon she added others, as godfathers and godmothers, to

* Bing. Ant., Vol. III. p. 552.

watch over the spiritual welfare of those who were yet lambs of the flock. That which was, in the first instance, assistant only to the office of the parent, became soon a distinct obligation. Our Church has adopted the result. She *forbids* parents to be sponsors. The caution, while it presumes the fidelity of the *natural* relationship, superadds that which represents only the *spiritual* obligation, and so at once distinguishes the spiritual nature of the New Birth, of which Baptism is the sign and external part and means, and secures the right direction of the efforts of parental love!

Do you acknowledge the wisdom and the suitableness of such an institution, so far as the first ages of the Church were concerned? I ask you, then, are there no reasons shewing it to be as wise and as suitable in the present day?

Do parents in the present day so effectually perform their promises respecting the religious education of their baptized children, in the large and proper sense of that term—parents among the rich as well as parents among the poor—that there is no need of the *assistant security* afforded by the obligations of the sponsors, if those obligations were indeed obeyed?

Do you ask me, then, what are the duties of a sponsor in the mixed state of things in which that office is assumed in the present day? You in effect ask me what the parent, as an enlightened member of the Church of England, who heartily concurs in her services, and who makes choice of the sponsor, in effect *concedes*, in respect of his office, if both the one and the other be indeed sincere.

His office, I answer, relates exclusively to the *reli-*

gious interests of the child, so far as they are involved in his education.

So long as the parent lives, the sponsor may not directly interfere with the education of the child.

But nothing is conceded to him, if he may not, with courtesy, as the apostle expresses it, supervise that education, so far as it affects the interest of the soul;— if he may not influence the course of it through the parent, and so co-mingle, as it were, his own affections for that end, with those of the natural guardians, educators and instructors of infancy.

Nor does the parent fulfil his duty in these respects, if he do not, as opportunity serves, take counsel with the sponsor; if he do not make known, as soon as may be, to the child, the Church-relationship which has been so created, in order that the influence of character in the sponsor may combine with his own advice and counsel to the end in view.

Then, as you know, all this is ultimately a *matter of grace* in the daily fulfilment (and there will certainly be a daily fulfilment) of the promises of God; and as the Church, as it were for more enlarged security, has connected prayer for its efficacy with the co-ordinate efficacy of the Sacrament, so, in the fulfilment of the conditions which rest on all the parties interested, prayer is the most efficacious of the *means* to be used. The great first duty, and, after ceaseless concurrence in all others, the last duty of the sponsor is earnest prayer to God for the child he represents, accompanied, as we have seen, by all possible and reasonable efforts, without which prayer is of no promised efficacy.

Do you, then, ask from me ministerial advice on this solemn and responsible subject?

I advise you never to undertake the office of Sponsor without, first of all, earnest prayer to God for his correction and guidance in that which is proposed to you. Ask that your way may be made plain before you.

Then, in like manner, satisfy yourself that, whether in measured forms or not, the parents do *intend* to devote their child to God in infancy and through life.

Require, in plain words require of them a right understanding, and, if possible, a concurrence respecting the intention of the Church service in Baptism, and the obligations consequently binding on all parties who unite therein, both the parents and yourself.

Claim permission, on the part of the parents, not uselessly to intermeddle in family regulations, or in the purposes and authority of the father and mother; but, as a sponsor, to watch kindly and courteously over the progress of religious education in the child;— to examine, to advise, and, as the times admirably serve, to place occasionally in his hands books of wise and suitable instruction. Let me here mention one book which has lately been put forth by the *Society for Promoting Christian Knowledge*, as, so far as it relates to this subject, admirably calculated to promote your views, and in all other respects as admirably instructive to all faithful members of the Church of England. I refer to the book entitled, " *The Liturgy compared with the Bible.*"

Then let it be your prayerful determination to keep ever and seriously in view the whole period between the Baptism of the child and his Confirmation. Let it be your ceaseless object to prepare him for that latter rite, and intend not to rest satisfied until by the public recognition of the Bishop, following upon his own sincere profession of faith and obedience, and accompanied by the earnest united prayers of the Church, the Bishop, the child and yourself, the blessings of the covenant which were assured to him in his Baptism, but in their larger and more personal measure hitherto suspended, are made his own.

I almost anticipate the thoughts which pass the minds, perhaps, of some now before me—"How can such things be?" "This is surely to follow out the subject beyond its possible limits." "Such days are gone by." "We must yield to the force of circumstances in the age in which we were born and live!"

The days of sincerity, that is, and of truth are gone by, and we must be content to be hypocrites and to mock God!

If the Church of England is to see better times, as, within the ordinary range of the life of those before me, I doubt not she will—if, that is, she is to become the efficient instrument of a large increase of vital religion in our country, it will be, not through the adoption of the varying fancies which are afloat respecting supposed errors in her doctrines, but through a cordial *renewal* of her discipline—and so far as we are concerned, that renewal must take its commencement in the proper recognition on the part of parents and of sponsors of their duties in respect of infants baptized into her society. When, in accordance with the services, parents and godfathers and godmothers begin to understand and to perform their duties to the infant members of the body of Christ, then brighter anticipations of the glory of the latter days will dawn upon us.

And here let me touch on a subject far, indeed, from being new, but which has been lately pressed on my attention, and on which I have cordially and gratefully reflected.

In the earlier ages of the Church, the office of Sponsor soon (as a question not of divine authority, but of wise and wholesome expediency) came to be regarded as, in a subordinate but most important sense, a church-office.* It was undertaken and followed out as a duty incumbent on those who desired as private Christians, and on principles of Christian charity, to promote the glory of the Saviour in the extension of his kingdom and the good of their fellow-creatures. Many of those who habitually partook of the Lord's Supper, felt themselves bound by this obligation. They did this, as you know, in times of ignorance and persecution, when the facilities of Christian instruction were comparatively few. We live in better days, wherein every means is offered to promote the religious education of children in all classes of society. The press—the school—the Church—all teem with truth, and it is negligence alone (if it be not something worse) which leaves the young in whom we are interested ignorant of that in which our present happiness and our eternal salvation are involved. Will the time be yet long delayed when we shall see

* Bing. Ant., Vol. III. p. 561.

righteous communicants acknowledging it as an obligation of Christian charity, themselves instructed in the truth and partakers of grace, to accept the office of sponsors to the children of the ignorant and uninstructed, with the clear understanding that they shall have liberty to watch the progress of religious education in those whom in this manner they have voluntarily undertaken to represent? Meditate on these things with seriousness, self-devotion, and prayer.

It remains to me now to realize to my mind the fact, that I have more than probably before me many persons who have, perhaps, frequently undertaken to fill the office of sponsor to children.

And, addressing myself to such, I would ask, Did no thought of self-reproach penetrate your mind when the announcement was just now read, that a Confirmation was shortly to be held for this parish, in this immediate neighbourhood?

The average number of Baptisms in this parish in each year is about 110. Of these, the average number of deaths in each year, between the birth and the age appointed for Confirmation, is thirty. Three years have now passed since that holy rite was administered in these parts. What, then, are the facts which are before us? Without regard to those who before neglected this paramount duty of the Christian, and they were many, the result in view of the last three years is this. There are 240 young persons who are of age to present themselves for instruction and examination by the appointed ministers of the Church, in order to their Confirmation; and, taking a large, and yet, I do

believe, strictly speaking, and in view of all to whom
it might apply, a very limited measure, there are at
this moment, in respect of this parish, 720 godfathers
and godmothers; and, if the order of the Church were
obeyed, adding to these the parents of the children,
(subject of course to all accidents which qualify num-
bers in such a case, and in a world of dying creatures,)
there are, on the whole, 1050 persons who are responsible to the Church and to God for the education in
the Christian faith of those for whom they undertook
to respond, and whom on the present occasion the
Church asks again at their hands.

Do no compunctions penetrate the hearts of such
persons?

I would again urge it upon you, that the office is
not of divine institution, and the undertaking of it
was therefore altogether voluntary on your part.

Have you, still to restrict myself to the sponsors,
either partially or altogether neglected your duty?
Then, advise with the parents—there are yet two
months before you. Bring the young persons under
the instruction of your appointed ministers. Assist
sedulously in that instruction yourselves. And from
this moment let' the conviction of your negligence
add vigour to other motives for earnest and persevering prayer, that the efforts so put forth may not be in
vain.

Addressing such persons, then, with the deepest
consciousness of the obligations to which I refer, and
with as deep ministerial affection, I will conclude my
discourse in the language suggested by my text. What
is required of parents and sponsors who have volun-

tarily, and in common, taken upon themselves the highest of Christian duties, with all the conditions and the promises attached to them—the religious education of the young—until, as now, they shall be presented to be examined as to their Christian attainments and character, and if found prepared for that rite, solemnly confirmed? What is required of them, but firmly and consistently to "stand to the covenant"?

I remind parents and sponsors, that on the next Sunday morning my address will be made to those who are to be presented to the Bishop for Confirmation.

And I remind them, too, that their fidelity will be put to the test by the number of names which shall be sent to the parochial ministers during the present week of young persons desirous of instruction and examination, in order to their being presented at the appointed time to the Bishop.

SERMON IV.

ADDRESS

TO

CANDIDATES FOR CONFIRMATION.

---

2 KINGS xxiii. 3:

And all the people stood to the covenant.

DEEPLY important as have been the subjects hitherto
submitted to our consideration during the course of
my Lectures on Confirmation, that on which I enter
this morning appeals to yet deeper feelings, and demands even yet more awakened attention than the rest.
I have attempted to throw light on the nature of the
sacred rite to which my Lectures more immediately
refer.   I have earnestly addressed, successively, the
parents and the sponsors of those who, with their
pledged concurrence, were devoted to God in Baptism in the earliest days of their infancy. This morning
my discourse contemplates *those of you who, having
been so baptized into the Church, are now of age to
make a public profession of your faith, and openly to*

claim the blessings which were then conditionally assured to you.

Is it possible to imagine a state which involves more solemnly-important considerations than, I will not say that which I have supposed, but that in which all those among you of suitable age, who are yet unconfirmed, do at this moment actually exist? The question is now put to you by the Church, "Will you stand to the covenant, of which you were made a party in the earliest days of your infancy?" And on the answer which your heart may return to that question are suspended your destinies for the eternal world.

A reluctant mind, deceived by the master-error of the present day, which *seems* to demand intellectual and moral liberty, but which the rather refuses to be made conscious of the necessarily painful removal of the galling chains of a corrupt nature, in order that it may truly be set free, may, even in youth, spurn from it the idea of religious obligation bound upon it in the infancy of life.

Do you then, indeed, imagine that natural liberty, whether in view of the intellect or the heart, in matters connected with your religious welfare, has any existence either in you or in others? Does life itself, bestowed upon you by your Creator, bring no responsibilities which are parallel to those which were bound upon you in your sponsors? Does it bear with it no original obligation to obey your parents' will, and, as time proceeds, to make the glory of God and your own everlasting interests the supreme objects of your existence? Can you escape from the judgment which

shall at the last be pronounced upon you in view
of the effect of education, or the circumstances or
relationships of life, or that you were born and have
been nurtured in a Christian country, in the midst of
Christian institutions, and with the examples of both
the evil and the good before you; and all this irrespectively of the obligations of Baptism, and altogether beyond your control? Men talk of liberty, but
who that lives can rid himself of responsibilities which
involve the everlasting welfare of his immortal soul!

So strongly, indeed, does this appeal to the natural
convictions of every man, that I doubt whether there
be an individual before me who, after a moment's reflection, would not feel himself bound to gratitude to
God, step by step, that he was born of Christian
parents, in a Christian country, to be subject to the
guiding influence of a Christian education, under the
guardian institutions of a Christian Church—all taking
their first efficiency to his spiritual benefit, so far as
he is personally concerned, in his being associated
with and united to the body of Christ by Baptism in
his infancy. And this is your actual state.

Let me, then, again remind you, that the Sacrament
of your Baptism took place wholly in that part of the
service which is according to the institution of our
Lord himself—the appointed use of water by him who
has authority to baptize, " in the name of the Father,
and of the Son, and of the Holy Ghost." All the rest
of the service has been arranged and is used at the
discretion of the Church. But, farther observe, that
in using that discretion it has been the Church's purpose, under guidance of Holy Scripture, to follow out

the principles, the grace and the obligations involved in the Sacrament, and so to construct the service as to make it in this view intelligible to all. It is true we were baptized according to the services of the Church of England, but that is only, in other words, to say, we were baptized in forms which were intended to be, and are, according to the principles of the Word of God. Had no other form been used but that which was instituted by the Lord, the same principles, so admirably followed out by the Church, would still have been necessarily, and to an equal extent, involved. The Baptism of infants, not now to speak of adults, involves the necessity, that is, of Confirmation. If it be needful that we should enter the Church of Christ by the Sacrament of Baptism, it is as needful that we should, in the progress of time and the establishment of our principles, *make personal confession of our faith, and claim the blessings of the covenant for ourselves.*

Against one prevalent error on this subject I will, at this point in my discourse, affectionately but earnestly warn those to whom I now more particularly address myself.

To ignorant and listless minds, which cannot brook the labour of accurate investigation and severe thought, hard terms and strong assertions serve for argument and the affirmation of truth. All which urges the necessity of forms and means to the edification of the body of Christ, is said by such persons to have had its origin in the Romish Church, and the mind is instantly prone to reject it as Popish. Whatever has had its origin in the errors of Rome, by all means reject; but be very careful lest, making the attempt in ignorance, you presumptuously uproot that which prevailed in the purer days of the Catholic Church before those errors had taken their origin, and which have their sanction, as the institutions of the Church of England, for the practical efficiency of the baptismal covenant, have their sanction, in the usages of the apostles themselves.

Then may I not?—I do most urgently—press on the consideration of the younger members of my flock, that it ill becomes them to form strong opinions, far less to rest upon or to be guided by any such opinions of their own, on subjects like these.

I am quite aware that this suggestion is in the present day, a day which is sinfully impatient of submission, judged to be antiquated and obsolete. But discipline will gradually return to us; and respect will be shewn by the young to the regulated religious authority of Christian parents, sponsors and the Church.

But are these, in truth, the reasons which prevail, perhaps, with many of the young persons of this parish, to withhold their names on the present occasion? Altogether the contrary. The negligence of parents and of sponsors has originated many such instances. And where Confirmation has been proposed to the young themselves, and they have refused to comply with the wish so expressed, or hesitate to present themselves to the Bishop, the reluctance has for the most part taken its rise in a secret conviction, that were they to conform in this instance to the institutions of the Church, they would be binding upon

themselves obligations to which they are not yet prepared to be subject.

Do you, then, intend—for the question is now put to
you—do you indeed intend to renounce, not the
sources of misery in this world and for ever, which
your sponsors at your Baptism promised you should
cordially renounce,—but do you now renounce your
faith in Christ, your allegiance to God, your privilege
of prayer, your interest in the means of grace; and
for the future are you content, through that renunciation, professedly to be to the Church as a heathen man
and a publican?

You have, in fact, no ultimate escape from such an
alternative. If you propose to stand to the covenant
of your Baptism, the Church now requires of you to
affirm in public your fidelity, and to receive permission
to claim a personal interest in her communion.

Happily, there are many of you, we have reason to
know, in whose hearts no such reluctance has place.
Now arrived at a suitable age, you earnestly desire to
recognize the obligations and secure the blessings of
your Baptism. To you, it is the most gratifying event
of life that you were early devoted to God, and that
from that moment to the present you have been under
the guardian care of those who have nurtured and
instructed you in the way of righteousness—unfolding
to you the truth as you were able to bear it—restraining you from evil, and by their example and wholesome authority leading you in obedience to the known
will of God.

You need no persuasion to the performance of a
duty which your religious education has ever disposed

you to believe to be paramount. You ask only an assurance from those who are appointed to be your public instructors, that you are in a state prepared for participation in the rite which is now before you.

To meet the wish so implied is my purpose in the present discourse, and in that which is to follow upon it on next Sunday morning.

I will endeavour to answer severally in these two discourses the following questions:

What is required by the Church of persons who present themselves to be confirmed?

And, *How must such persons subsequently guide their conduct, in order that, to use the language of the Church, they may continue to be the children of God for ever, and daily increase in his Holy Spirit more and more, until they come into his everlasting kingdom?*

In entering to-day on the former of these subjects, I perceive at once the necessity of restricting myself to principles. The subject is itself too large for the limits of a public discourse; and, moreover, the particulars of which it is formed are more suitable for the private and personal instruction and examination of the appointed ministers, which must precede the grant of permission on our part, that you should on the present occasion present yourselves to the Bishop to be confirmed.

We ask, then, in general terms, what is that state of mind, indicative of religious attainments and character, which the Church regards as requisite to Confirmation by the Bishop?

It is involved in the answer to the affecting question, then to be addressed to you,

"Do ye here, in the presence of God and of this congregation, renew the solemn promise and vow that was made in your name at your Baptism; ratifying and confirming the same in your own persons, and acknowledging yourselves bound to believe and to do all those things which your godfathers and godmothers then undertook for you?"

The requisite state of mind expresses itself in the simple response—"I do."

What those few but pregnant words intend, must be discovered by careful comparison of the Baptismal Service, the Service for Confirmation, and the Catechism, *with each other, and all and several of these with the inspired Word of God.*

Without attempting, on the present occasion, to follow out this comparison, I may content myself with observing that,

In the first place, the Church requires of you *adequate knowledge* of the great principles and forms of truth and Christian obligation. She is not like the heretical Church of Rome, which nourishes ignorance in her members in order that she may enforce her doctrine of tyranny in the hands of her priesthood— that, regardless of the administrator and of the recipient, there is a necessary effect of that which she ministers. The Church of England begins with the birth— appoints pledged instructors—and when their work of education and instruction is completed, examines and receives her enlightened members into full communion.

Time, I have said, will not permit me now to enter into the particulars of knowledge which she thus requires.

It is for you, candidates for Confirmation, to pass the period still allowed to you in serious study of these matters. Compare diligently the services to which I have referred in all their parts, and with an unprejudiced mind, with each other and with Holy Scripture. The newly-published book which I recommended to your notice last Sunday—I speak of the work entitled, "The Liturgy compared with the Bible"—will greatly assist you in this. Presume not that you are already acquainted with these things. You may, as we express it, know the Catechism by heart, and yet remain in ignorance respecting them. The oldest student needs yet to persevere. Step by step, search out the thoughts there suggested to you, and confirm what you know by large illustrations from the Word of God. So occupy yourself until the appointed day. Let it be a duty of secret hours, but in difficulties seek the aid of your parents, your sponsors, or your ministers. Ignorance will dispose you to presume the existence of adequate knowledge. Inquiry opens to us our deficiencies, and perhaps leads us to the conviction suggested by the apostle, that we know "nothing yet as we ought to know."

But we are in much danger of resting here. There are many, it is to be feared, who have an adequate knowledge of the truths and obligations of religion, without any consistent impression of its power.

In addition, then, to knowledge, the Church requires of you *a living and effectual faith in all which the*

Gospel sets before you. "ALL THIS I STEADFASTLY BELIEVE." And by faith she intends, not a mere cold assent of the understanding, but, what the Bible intends in that term, such a conviction as may move and regulate the heart and the life—a faith which worketh by love—a faith which is not dead, being alone, but living and fruit-bearing.

And the subjects of religious knowledge are the field over which a living faith has its range. Observe, then, that the examination of your minister is of little benefit to you, without a previous and concurrent *self*-examination on your part—a self-examination that contemplates all which knowledge throws open before your mind. Is this, then, an occasion for renewing and enlarging your knowledge? As each point passes under review, secretly inquire of your heart whether you so believe it as to make it a governing principle of your life; all, for instance, which the Word of God affirms respecting yourself, your Saviour, the guidance and aid of the Holy Spirit, your conduct in the present world, and your hopes or fears in the next. Do you truly, that is feelingly and practically, believe all these things?

The Church farther requires of you the disposition humbly, but cheerfully, to *submit yourself to and obey* the known will of God.

It is true, that for conciseness she sums up the particulars of that obedience in the compendium of the moral law included in the Ten Commandments, but she is far from restricting our obligations thereto. Rightly interpreted under the light of the Gospel, they offer to us the germ of all we owe to God and to

our neighbours; and in pledging our submission to
them, we do in truth take the whole revealed will of
God for the law of our life. On these two, love to
God and love to our neighbour, hang all the law and
the prophets.

Another field of self-inquiry is thus thrown open
before us. Knowledge contemplates the rules of action
as well as the principles which dispose us to obedience. Are you, then, in search of knowledge to prepare you for the holy rite? Take each requirement
into the chamber of your heart. Are you there (the
book of Revelation open before you) in sincerity addressing the inquiry to the throne of heaven,—Lord,
what wilt thou have me to do? *Knowledge recognizes* the law and ascribes to it the authority of God.
Obedience makes use of that which is so recognized as
a rule of submission and of action. Has *your* religion
led you thus far? Are you sincerely adopting for
yourselves the pledge once given by your sponsors on
your behalf—" At this moment my heart is fixed. *I
will obediently keep God's holy will and commandments, and walk in the same all the days of my life"*?

The Church requires more of you. She looks for
*a cordial renunciation of all sin, and a purpose to
resist all temptations to iniquity.*

It is after contemplating the inner seeds and elements of evil, the pageantry of the vain world, and
the dominion of that base spirit whose whole being is
imbued with iniquity, and whose every purpose is the
dishonour of God and the destruction of souls,—with
these in view, the sincere servant of his Lord, asking
confirmation of his privileged communion with the

Church, is supposed and required to adopt the thrilling affirmation of his sponsors—I RENOUNCE THEM ALL! Do these words express the deep and sincere feeling of your hearts? Are you ready, now and for evermore, to break allegiance with the prince of the darkness of this world? Are all the vanities of life fading from your view? Have you already commenced the inward and deeply-felt struggle with the law which is in your members warring against the law of your mind? To all this does your heart sincerely respond—I renounce them all! From this time forward I serve not Satan, not the world, not the lusts of my own heart, but wholly and alone the Lord Christ!

Again, the Church expects in those who are confirmed a *deep sense of their inability, of themselves, to believe and to do that which is required of those who would partake of the blessings of the Gospel.* "THOU ART NOT ABLE TO DO THESE THINGS OF THYSELF." Thou canst not of the natural power of thine intellect believe all which thou hast attained to know. Thou canst not of the strength of thy natural will either awaken good desires in thy heart, or carry out those desires into good effect. Now this also is either a subject of knowledge, or an inward deep-felt conviction of the heart. Is that conviction yours? Does the commandment of God appear to you exceeding broad, and do his promises seem as exceedingly desirable, and yet you feel your inability so to obey the one as to secure to yourself the other? The value of a Saviour—the wisdom of the economy of our salvation—the daily aid of the Holy Spirit—all these things we estimate as we are sensible of our own unprofitableness. "What the law could not do in that it was weak through the flesh, God, sending his own Son in the likeness of sinful flesh, and for sin, condemned sin in the flesh, that the righteousness of the law might be fulfilled in us, who walk not after the flesh, but after the Spirit." All this you know. Is your knowledge intimate—the knowledge of consciousness—awakening in your soul, in forms of self-reproach, humiliation, penitence, desire of the full and perfect atonement of the Saviour, dependance, a hope which lays hold of that which is within the veil?

This the Church requires of you—an inward feeling of the truth—I can do none of these things of myself!

The Church, nevertheless, looks for *a holy but dependant resolution to put forth the effort, which must derive its efficacy from above.* "YES, VERILY, AND BY GOD'S HELP, SO I WILL."

It belongs to true religion to attempt what it is impossible to perfect, and so to do what it can effect, although it cannot reach to the bounds of the desires of the heart. And there is a wide difference between this and self-confidence. He who affects to know himself, and forms holy resolutions in reliance on his own strength, is a self-deceiver; but it is of faith, and it is the most sure evidence of the Christian efficiency of our belief, with the eye of the mind intently fixed on our utter inability to do any thing which is well-pleasing to God, yet to make firm resolutions, and follow out those resolves into action, *dependant on the grace of God:* for true religion recognizes not only what we ought to do, but the promise of assistance also if we make the attempt.

I repeat it, then, have you this pledge of the sincerity with which you purpose to offer yourself for Confirmation, that you have truly *resolved*, by God's grace, from this moment to renew the purposes of your parents at your Baptism, and, now, to devote yourself to God?

It is this which on your part gives truth and efficacy to the rite of which you are about to partake. Examine, then, I beseech you, the motives which prevail in your heart. Is it your understanding alone which assents, or have you indeed full purpose of mind in accordance with that to which with your lips you intend to give response?

Farther, to assist you in your inquiry into the fitness of your actual state for participation in this holy rite, the Church looks forward to the future, and presumes that the spirit by which you are now moved has in it that which will CONTINUE THE SAME UNTO YOUR LIFE'S END.

Never was there a worse fallacy than in the thought that Confirmation is a *terminating* service—a sign that, religious education being now complete, the confirmed may for the future guide himself by his own discretion, and even defer to some future time the more marked obligations of the faith which he thus professes. Rather, on the contrary, is it the *beginning* of a renewed life. Hitherto the Church has looked upon you as under the guidance of others. Now she expects that you should begin to take your place among those who, in all right principle and holy purpose, are going onward to perfection.

Realize the solemn service to your mind. You are

about to stand in the presence of your parents, your sponsors, the minister who has examined you, the Church, the Bishop by whom the Confirmation is to take place, and God, the great Searcher of hearts, with the book of Revelation open, as it were, before you, and well knowing all which, in accordance with the principles of that changeless record of the Divine purposes and will, has been promised and claimed for you. You are about to acknowledge yourself no longer your own, but bought with a price—the precious blood of your Saviour. You are about to affirm the sincerity of your purpose and desire to continue, in holy obedience and love, the child of God for ever. You are about to appeal to your actual state—your heart as seen by the all-wise God—as an assurance that you are sincere, and, in order to avoid all suspicion of possible duplicity, to express your mind in the simplest terms—" I DO." All this is shortly to pass. And is there indeed to be, as uttered by you, something of spiritual, something of eternal life in those words? Or shall they be the concentrated expression of hypocrisy, deceit, inward rejection of the Saviour, despite of the Spirit of God, daring mockery of the Most High, recklessness of the loss of your soul? Will you fearlessly and carelessly repeat the words of acknowledged obligation; claim, in letter, the blessings of the Gospel, and then go back to your home and to your ordinary occupations, still under the dominion of sin, a lover of the world, a slave of passion, wearing the badge of your profession without any due influence from its grace, to live without God in this world, and having no hope for the next!

The Church requires of you an acknowledgment that the service of Confirmation is a renewal of the living energy of a holy life, to be continued throughout your existence in this world, and merged at last in that of eternity.

One other indication of a prepared state she requires —*sincere, heartfelt, persevering prayer.* HIS SPECIAL GRACE THOU MUST LEARN AT ALL TIMES TO CALL FOR BY DILIGENT PRAYER.

We have not a right view of that which the Gospel throws open before us—our sinfulness; our inability to do any thing acceptable to God ; the binding nature of our responsibilities; the exceeding holiness of the law ; the fearful issues which are suspended on our obedience ; the provision which is made for our restoration to the favour of God, and the renewal of our heart and life by the grace of the Holy Spirit, and after the image of him who is " the first-born among many brethren;"—the proffered recognition of all these things is ineffectual of any good result, unless it move us to earnest and continuous prayer. Desiring, fearing, hoping, distrusting ourselves, and yet resolved by the promised grace of God, these things we must call for by diligent prayer.

The Church, then, does not ask of you alone, What is the measure of your knowledge ?—what have you resolved ?—what is the direction of your desires and your efforts ?—but, For what do you in your secret heart and habitually pray ? There is no life in knowledge, no sincerity in desire, no purpose in resolution, no dependance in faith, no holiness, no hope without prayer.

In this, then, I conclude my address to you for this morning.

Recognize the propriety of your wish now to present yourselves to the Bishop to be confirmed, in the measure of the spirit of prayer of which you are conscious. Then pray earnestly to God to give you his grace to aid you in the necessary previous duty of self-examination—to discover your actual state —your preparedness or your want of preparation for that holy rite. Pray as earnestly that the blessing of God may rest on your parents, your sponsors and your ministers, in the advice and instruction which, in the course of their inquiry into your fitness, they may give to you. Pray for the Holy Spirit to give a right direction and force to all the movements of your mind in view of what is before you. Pray for the Divine presence when you may offer yourselves before the Church for the purpose you have in view—his presence recognizing and blessing the congregation, the Bishop, and especially yourself. That which is thus begun in prayer will issue in holiness and be prolonged to eternal life.

To what have I thus far advised you, but in sincerity, firmness of purpose, dependance on the grace of God, and assurance of his faithfulness, to " stand to the covenant" ?

SERMON V.

ADDRESS

TO

CANDIDATES FOR CONFIRMATION.

2 Kings xxiii. 3:

And all the people stood to the covenant.

I FIND it needful, in entering on this second part of my Address to *the Candidates for Confirmation*, in order to prevent all misconception of what I may think it my duty to bring under their notice, to state again, as plainly as I may, the limits which are prescribed to me.

I presume, then, that I have before me enlightened and faithful members of the Church of England ; not those who attend the services of the Church because habits early formed so dispose them, or because they have not yet come to the conclusion that she ought to be deserted by them, or because they have never made this a matter of serious examination, and have by consequence no fixed principles respecting it,—but those who from conviction, and cordially, surrender themselves to her institutions and submit to her rule.

With the course which others pursue, I claim no right, and I am sensible of no disposition, to inter-meddle. But deeply and inwardly should I be con-victed of guilty reserve, if, with the purpose of con-ciliating those whom I know to be in error, I were to withhold from the candidates for Confirmation and others of you to whom I immediately address myself, a plain statement of that which I equally know to be ac-cording to the truth.

My obligation, indeed, to state, without reservation, the requirements of the truth, is, if possible, the more stringent on the present occasion. "If the trumpet give an uncertain sound, who shall prepare himself for the battle?" The want of definiteness, and there-fore the changeful inconsistency of principle and of conduct, among those who call themselves Christians, which is characteristic of our day, is properly to be traced to the doubtfulness of religious instruction under which generations have now been born and passed away. The sin of insubordination has thus become as familiar to us as the first elements of thought by which our principles are formed and our life is guided.

I address myself directly, moreover, to those who are candidates to partake of a rite which, in this coun-try and in this our day, though not in view of the universal church and of the earliest periods of the Gospel, is peculiar to the Church of England; and who therefore acknowledge themselves bound, not only, though supremely, to that which Holy Scripture requires of them to believe and to do for their soul's health,—but subordinately, yet with equal sincerity, to the services which the Church has set forth as at once explanatory and in strict obedience to what is stated and enforced in the inspired Word of God.

What the Church requires of such persons in order to Confirmation, I have already attempted to unfold.

WHAT THE CHURCH HOPES AND DEMANDS OF SUCH PERSONS AFTER CONFIRMATION, is this morning to form the subject of my discourse.

I shall construct my sermon, then, very much in the form of advice for the guidance of the conduct of those of this parish whom the Bishop shall, on our certificate of their due preparation, receive, examine, pray for and bless, in the name of the Father, and of the Son, and of the Holy Ghost.

And to such persons I may perhaps best commence my Address by directing their attention to the form of words, in the use of which, as an earnest prayer, with the laying on of hands, Confirmation takes place :

" *Defend, O Lord, this thy child (or this thy servant) with thy heavenly grace, that he may continue thine for ever, and daily increase in thy Holy Spirit more and more, until he come unto thy everlasting kingdom.*"

Now observe. There is no part of religious obligation more essentially practical than prayer. We ask for grace to *enable us to be obedient* to the will of God, for his glory and our own spiritual and eternal welfare—we ask, sincerely purposing both to seek and, if attained, to concur in the sacred tendencies of that which may be bestowed upon us—or else we pray not at all.

We might apply this to the prayer for Confirmation which I have cited, and, without further remark, change its several clauses into the form of exhortation and advice to those who have been confirmed. First, however, let us turn our attention to the prayers which immediately follow upon, and are therefore intended to be farther explanatory of the mind of the Church in her supplications for those who are now introduced into the full enjoyment of her privileges.

I pass over, for the present, the Lord's Prayer, which is strongly illustrative of the principle affirmed, and restrict myself to the two Collects of which the rest of the service is composed. There, too, have we supplications for grace—but how expressed?

"*Almighty and Everlasting God, who makest us* BOTH TO WILL AND TO DO *those things which are good and acceptable unto thy Divine Majesty*——*let thy Holy Spirit ever be with these thy servants, and so* LEAD *them in the* KNOWLEDGE AND OBEDIENCE *of thy word,* that in the end they may obtain everlasting life."

And again, "*Vouchsafe so to* DIRECT, SANCTIFY *and* GOVERN, BOTH OUR HEARTS AND BODIES IN THE WAYS OF THY LAWS, AND IN THE WORKS OF THY COM- MANDMENTS, *that through thy most mighty protection, both here and ever, we may be preserved in body and soul, through our Lord and Saviour Jesus Christ.*"

The primary desire expressed in these prayers is manifestly for the gift of the Spirit; but the gift of that Spirit is sought for truly practical ends—to stir up the mind to the right pursuit of heavenly things, and to make effectual the dispositions and the energies so awakened to the attainment of faith and holiness in the present life, and eternal happiness in the next.

In addressing you, then, in respect of the obligations which the Church regards as binding upon you for ever *after*, and in respect of, your Confirmation, I will arrange what I may have to say under the several clauses expressed or implied in the prayer offered by the Bishop when administering the sacred rite.

First, then, *Let the primary, the ruling principle of your subsequent religious life be in the thought that you are a* CHILD,—A SERVANT OF GOD.

We are, indeed, to pray for all men—even for those who are far out of the pale—even persecutors of the Church of Christ; but for those only who are acknowledged members of that holy body could words be addressed to heaven, like those of the introduction to this prayer. THIS, for whom we pray, is THY CHILD— THY SERVANT.

And there is here no vain presumption. Was your Baptism, in one important view, regarded as the first devotion of your life to the service of God — your admission into the family of Christ for instant education, and, as your powers should open, instruction after his will, in dependance on the promised aid of his Spirit? Were you thus declared a CHILD OF God in faith of the efficacy of that which even then took its commencement? You have at your Confirmation declared that your judgment, your heart and your conscience concur in all this, and you have claimed for yourself the acknowledged privileges of a child of God! On your own profession—on your ratification of the vows of your Baptism, we recognize you as such. From this time forth, then, let this be the dominant thought of your mind—I AM A CHILD— I am a SERVANT of God!

The practical unfolding of this principle is the subject of the other clauses of the prayer; but how valuable is the acknowledgment of the principle itself!

Henceforth, if you are indeed sincere in all you have professed of faith and obedience, the Church publicly recognizes the fact, that the guilt and the fatal consequences, for this world and the next, of the corruption of your nature which you inherited from your fallen progenitor Adam, have passed away; that you have a living and effectual interest in the cross of your Redeemer; that the blood of Jesus Christ, the Son of God, has cleansed you from all sin; that the gracious promises of the Word of God, adapted as they are to all the varying conditions of the Christian's state, and bestowed through the all-deserving Head to the still-undeserving body, the Church, are held in store for you; that you have the gift of the Holy Ghost, for all the ends of a holy and a hopeful life. To you, who have thus received the Saviour, God Most High has given power to become his child, through faith in his name.

In this large view, let the ruling thought within you be ever this—"I am a child of God—a servant of his will. Truth is addressed, grace is offered to the worldly as to aliens from the commonwealth of Israel, and strangers to the covenant of promise ; but to me they are held forth as to a child reconciled to my Heavenly Father in Christ Jesus. Obedience is exacted of them as in view of all the obligations of an offended law, and all the suspended penalties which justice is even now prepared to enforce ; but of me, as of one whom his Father loves, and in contemplation of the favour, promises and grace of the better covenant," " What shall we say then ? Shall we continue in sin that grace may abound ? God forbid ! How shall we that are dead in sin, live any longer therein ? Know ye not that so many of us as were baptized into Jesus Christ were baptized into his death ? Therefore we are buried with him by Baptism into death ; that like as Christ was raised up from the dead by the glory of the Father, even so we also should walk in newness of life."

Never, then, forget this your new relationship, openly commenced at your Baptism, and confessed and ratified at your Confirmation. The mental repose, the confidence, the cheerful and ready obedience of a child to his parent, concentrate in the *filial affection* of his heart. Let your mental repose, your holy dependance on God, your free and full obedience to all his known will as revealed throughout his word, have their abiding-place and their living service in the Spirit that dwells ever within you—the glow of a holy affection which ascends upward to the presence of the Most High, and there expresses the deepest desires of the soul in the language of a child-like confidence and love—Abba ! Father !

Then, *Look to your Heavenly Father, in and through the Lord Jesus Christ, for* DEFENCE against all the dangers of your religious course. " DEFEND, O LORD, THIS THY CHILD."

We have on a former occasion observed, that all resolutions of good made in dependance on ourselves, are but a vain mockery offered to the Most High. Sin has brought upon us an utter inability to do that which is pleasing and acceptable to God. The prayers which compose the service of Confirmation, we have seen, imply the same.

We may, for instance, in truth and sincerity, at the present moment affirm our full belief in God's Word, our readiness to submit ourselves to the obligations of his law, and our cordial renunciation of the world, the flesh and the devil. But have we power to preserve alive for one succeeding moment the spark of grace which is within us? When it has subsided and is apparently quenched, can we renew the hidden energy and fan it to a flame?

Alas! no sooner shall the words and the prayers of Confirmation have passed—words of affirmation and resolve on your part, and words of holy intercession and blessing from him who is appointed to minister the rite, than the contest with evil will be renewed. You will carry away with you from the house and presence of God a sinful nature, prone to wander from him who hath bought you with his blood. The law which is in your members will still and fiercely war against the law which is in your mind. You will return to worldly concerns, which are divided by a narrow line alone from those of unblushing iniquity.

You will, perhaps of necessity of relationship, go back to those who are prepared to lead you into all the gaieties of a vain and deceitful life. The prince of the power of the air will be instantly, as he will be continuously, waiting to snatch the holy seed from your heart, or, by devices numberless, to nip its growth, or effectually check its productiveness, and make you barren of the results of the grace of God.

You believe now, it may be, with the brightness of an inward and undisturbed conviction—who shall say that from some unexpected quarter the dark cloud of infidelity shall not arise and gradually veil your mind in the obscurity of unresisted error?

Your resolution to devote yourself to the one service of God, is now, perhaps, without qualification. Are you sure that no after-thoughts of listlessness shall be suggested, and your energy shall not subside into coldness and indifference?

If, indeed, you are rightly impressed with the obligation of this holy rite, you inwardly tremble when such thoughts are made to pass before you.

How suitably does the Church guide your resolutions which she encourages you to express!

Dost thou *renew the solemn promise and vow that was made in thy name at thy Baptism?*

I DO.

OUR HELP, she adds, IS IN THE NAME OF THE LORD.

Happily, evil, and the *returning* suggestions of evil, assume not *suddenly* supremacy of power over the mind. Temptation leaves time for prayer. A consciousness of our own infirmities is the very position in which the soul supplicates divine aid.

Never, then, let the thought escape you, that in God is your defence. As it were by a holy habit of mind, flee for succour, when the sound of danger first awakens on your ear, to " the covert of his wing." Build up your hopes on the truth affirmed to the apostle, " My grace is sufficient for thee; for my strength is made perfect in weakness." Be sincere. Think faithfully of this, and then, like the apostle in the midst of all dangers, you shall be able to say, " I take pleasure in infirmities, in reproaches, in necessities, in persecutions, in distresses for Christ's sake; for when I am weak, then am I strong."

Next, in accordance with the expectations of the Church respecting you after Confirmation, I advise you,—*In the steady and persevering use of* THE MEANS *for the attainment of the grace of God, let it be your object to* CONTINUE *to be the child of God to the end.*

So the Church prays for you—that, defended *by his* HEAVENLY GRACE *you may* CONTINUE *to be his for ever.*

Bear ever in mind, then, that it is of God's grace alone that you have any desire or ability to believe in and serve him. That grace has brought you, if, indeed, you are sincere, now openly to profess your faith in him, and your desire and purpose to be obedient to all the obligations of his Gospel. That grace, too, can alone make your holy resolutions effectual through the various means which he has appointed to this end; and to this end those means must be continually used.

Be careful never to neglect the private and personal

duties, which are the more intimate means of grace in the continuance of a religious life.

Let no day pass without devotional study of some portion, short as it may be, of the Word of God. " Read, mark, learn and inwardly digest" what there unfolds itself before you.

Set apart a fixed period of every morning and evening for meditation, prayer and praise. These are the links in the chain which connects the commencement with the issues of faith and obedience.

Regulate your whole life—every arrangement, every pursuit—by the principles of the Word of God, that through every event of your existence some good may be derived to your spiritual and eternal interests.

Carry your religion into your heart—make that your cherished oratory. Thither let all your powers of reflection and adoration frequently retire. There first transact with God, the Church, the world and yourself, the great business of your salvation. There renew your penitence, your faith and your obedience. Look to the past, the present and the future, and, with judgment to the line and righteousness to the plummet, fathom the depths of principle and of thought.

Then come forth into life again. Bring with you the seeds of holiness. Be in fact, what in language you so freely profess—a Christian, after the example of your risen Lord. Take your religion with you into business; into society; into all the movements of home; and all the stirring scenes of which each of us forms a part. " Whatsoever things are true, whatsoever things are honest, whatsoever things are just, whatsoever things are pure, whatsoever things are lovely, whatsoever things are of good report,—if there be any virtue, and if there be any praise, think on these things. Those things which ye have learned and received and heard, and, through the writings of apostolic men, have seen in them, do, and the God of peace shall be with you."

But I forget not that the great blessing of your Confirmation is the cementing, as it were, of your communion with the Church, for all the blessings which God has bestowed upon and secured to her in Christ. What I have said, then, of *private* and *personal* duties as means of grace to you, may with equal force be urged in reference to all the obligations of *communion* with the saints of God.

Frequently have I, throughout my discourses on Confirmation, endeavoured to trace the distinction between that which is of direct scriptural injunction, and therefore, even in respect of its form, of immediate divine authority, and that which is of the discretion entrusted to the Church, for the edification of her members; not of directly divine authority, indeed, but unquestionably binding upon and beneficial to those who concur in the institution of them, and believe that they are truly derived from and grounded upon Scripture principles. To such, (and such are all those who are, of their own choice, confirmed according to the modes of the Church,) her doctrine and *her discipline—her discipline* not the less than her doctrine—are effectual means of edification.

You believe that God is not a God of confusion, but of order. You conscientiously perceive that

without order there is no edification, and that order
and discipline you recognize in the institutions of the
Church. She is your acknowledged guide in the
observance of the Sabbath, in the services of God's
house, in the arrangements of worship, in the reading
and hearing of God's Word. Distinctly and properly
as these may be, of their own nature and in themselves, means of grace, they are so *to you* after the
manner in which the Church ministers them. You
judge not others—why should you? To their own
Master they stand or fall. But, instructed as you are,
the means of your edification are arranged for you
according to the discipline of the Church of England.
Most earnestly do I advise you with all unchanging
strictness to adhere to that discipline.

There are enough in the present day to tell you that
it is of little consequence where you go, and according to what form you worship, so that you hear that
which commends itself to your individual mind and
feelings as the Gospel of Christ. Discipline, that is,
they would seem to say, on the one hand, and submission for edification on the other, are matters of
individual taste.

Now I warn you seriously against both the example and the advice of such persons.

I do sincerely respect those who, having, from
whatever cause, fallen into the error of believing that
the discipline of the Church of England is not according to the Word of God, do charitably, but consistently, altogether avoid and absent themselves from
her services, and attend to other modes of edification.
But fearful indeed appears to be the state of others

who, thinking these to be matters of no importance, encourage, as well by their example as by their words, that spirit of confusion which is so prevalent in the present day.

Quench within your heart, I beseech you, an unholy desire of novelty and excitement. Deceive not yourself by the imagination that a spirit which has broken loose from wholesome restraint, and justifies itself in a resistance to control, by holding that modes of discipline are of minor importance, is a spirit of Christian charity and love; but rather gratefully and perseveringly, and soberly too, and in the fear of God, make use of the ordered means of your edification which the Church has provided for you.

And, therefore, let nothing hinder you from an early and an unceasing participation OF THE SACRAMENT OF THE LORD'S SUPPER—a means of grace as it is—the pledge of the efficiency of all other means—a bond of communion—an occasion, frequently recurring, inwardly to renew, and openly to profess and seal, that covenant by which you have, with purpose of heart, surrendered yourself to be the Lord's.

But, farther, in the prayer of Confirmation the Church seems to admonish you that it is of the nature of a justifiable assurance of the favour of God, that your religion be *in every respect* PROGRESSIVE. May he DAILY INCREASE IN THY HOLY SPIRIT MORE AND MORE!

The words are strikingly impressive. They intend, no doubt, the same as those of the apostle, addressed to us in the form of exhortation—" Grow in grace." All grace is from the Spirit of God, who bestows it upon us, dwelling himself in the heart, and thereby manifesting his presence and his sanctifying power through the various means which he has appointed thereto. In the passage to which we have referred, growth in grace is said to accompany growth in knowledge of the Lord and Saviour. In other parts of Scripture, its increase is set forth as fruitful in the larger attainment of other Christian virtues: we are babes in Christ before we reach to manhood and to the maturity of the spiritual life.

Acknowledge this, then, practically. Be it your supreme object to *abound* more and more in every good word and work. Daily, by watchfulness, self-denial, diligence and prayer, "add to your faith virtue, and to virtue knowledge, and to knowledge temperance, and to temperance patience, and to patience godliness, and to godliness brotherly kindness, and to brotherly kindness charity: for if these things be in you and *abound*, they make you that ye shall neither be barren nor unfruitful in the knowledge of our Lord Jesus Christ."

The spirit of true religion in the soul is restless of its present state and acquirements. It aspires to something more adequate to the demands of the law—more accordant with the example of the Saviour—more unreservedly obedient to the new affections which glow upon the heart. "Know ye not that they which run in a race run all, but one receiveth the prize? So run, then, that ye may obtain."

But this borders on the last topic of advice to which the Church invites our attention by this prayer, and to which I will very shortly, in conclusion, refer. She looks that the confirmed *live in anticipation of the eternal issue of their faith and obedience*—UNTIL HE COME UNTO THINE EVERLASTING KINGDOM.

For you have limited views of your Confirmation unless you connect it with your everlasting welfare.

For the future, then, conduct your life in anticipation of the perfections and the glories of another world. Live, not by sight, but by faith. Look, not at the things which are seen, which are temporal, but at the things which are not seen, which are eternal. Be urged forward to all which is good, be restrained from all which is evil, be moved to unceasing and intense interest in the things which are profitable to your salvation, by an inward but supreme gratitude to your Lord, and a sincere love of his appearing. And let the thought keep watch at the door of your heart—let it present itself there with the dawn of the morning—let it guard every movement of your soul, every word of your lips, and every action of your life, during the day—let its form fade on your perceptions only when you surrender yourself to the repose of the night—"Yet a little while, and he that shall come will come, and will not tarry." Meanwhile, "the just shall live by his faith;"—"but if any man draw back," his Lord, at his coming, "shall have no pleasure in him."

"Stand" faithfully, then, and perseveringly, "to the covenant," if you desire to hail the appearance of your Lord with joy, and with him enter into his promised glories in heaven!

SERMON VI.

COMMON AND MUTUAL OBLIGATIONS

OF THOSE WHO ARE

CONFIRMED MEMBERS OF THE CHURCH.

2 KINGS xxiii. 3:

And all the people stood to the covenant.

IN my five preceding Discourses on Confirmation, I
have endeavoured to occupy the attention of the members of this congregation who are more immediately
interested in the approaching administration of that
sacred rite. I now address those of you who have
already partaken of it, and are therefore presumed
to be in the enjoyment of the privileges, and, by
profession and acknowledgment on your part,
bound by the duties which it at once assures and
enjoins. As the Bishop has prescribed the sixteenth
year as suitable for Confirmation, may I not hope that
all persons before me above that age will listen to
my discourse as especially contemplating themselves?
That *personal* application of what may be said, I
am desirous, in the first instance, to encourage.

There is, perhaps, nothing more difficult, because it is opposed to the ordinary habit and current of our thoughts, than to realize and seriously contemplate in all their bearings, our actual relationships with God and our fellow-creatures. Of what we are, as intellectual and sentient beings, we are, perhaps, immediately conscious. But of what we are—what are our privileges and what our obligations, in the relationships of life, as they become more remote from our original consciousness, men scarcely care to inquire.

It is, on this account, of the first importance to inquire accurately into the nature of THE CHRISTIAN CHURCH, and to propose to ourselves, as an attainment of the highest practical value, to discover what is involved in *membership* of that holy communion. What do we intend when we say—I am a member of the Church of Christ? or, I am a member of the Church of England, which is a part of the visible Church of Christ?

Now the term which we render " Church" is used in the Scriptures in various senses. To all of these it is not needful to my present purpose to refer.

So far as we are immediately concerned it intends, a society or assembly of persons *called out*, as the original term intends, from the rest, and at once contradistinguished from them and associated together by certain divine laws, institutions, privileges and duties, and all these for certain ends, divinely purposed and definitely understood.

That in the term Church, reference is distinctly made to the *calling* of her members, the *primary idea* of a Church seems to contemplate the state of the society of which we have spoken, in the present world, as contradistinguished from that of her members, before they had attended to the Gospel invitation, and of those who still remain in their unregenerate condition. But in view of *the end* for which that calling takes place, and the only source of the efficiency of the means which are appointed to be used for that end, *the idea* of the Church limits itself to those who are sincerely obedient to the truth in the present world, and those who are in the enjoyment of the fruits of the great propitiation in the next.

On the whole, the definition of the Church may be made to include all who *are called* in the *visible* world, and all who *are glorified* in that which is *invisible:* or, it may be restricted to that which is visible here: or, it may be yet farther limited, for reasons hereafter to be alleged, to the members of the great community which may be associated under distinct laws and modes of discipline in nations, in districts, in congregations, in households; but never in such sense as to imply a disruption or separation from the unity of the whole; the minor divisions are always included under, merged in, and form an essential part of that by which it is territorially embraced, until the earthly limits be those of the world, and the whole range of her community be regarded as the whole number of the faithful.*

The ideas of this subject in which we are for the present the most interested, and which bear most intimately on that which is now before us, are those of the *universal* Church in this world, and of our *national*

* Eph. v. 23—27; Col. i. 24; 1 Cor. xvi. 19; Acts xx. 17; Rev. ii. 1; 1 Cor. xiv. 23; Rom. xvi. 5; Heb. xii. 22—24.

Church as an integral part of it—or the Church, whether by that term we intend the whole or a distinct part,
as subjected and presenting itself to the limited per-
ception of human beings, and therefore called *visible*.

And, still to restrict ourselves for one moment to
the intention of the *name* by which this community is
designated, and as introductory to what I may have
farther to offer, it would appear to be primary to the
idea of a Church as existing in the present world, that
it has been divinely instituted, in the first place, for
the CALLING of men out of the world to the Saviour,
and then, for the gradual preparation of those so
called, through the sympathies and the energies of the
body into which they are so brought, for the final con-
summation of the Divine will respecting those who
believe in, love and obey him, in another world.
CALLING, then, and EDIFICATION are the great objects
proposed to the Church of God on earth, whether
regarded in its undivided unity or in its subordinate
divisions.

What does this necessarily imply, but that the
Church is the province of Divine grace for the discipline and education for eternal life of all who are
included within her pale, and that from her goes forth
the warning and the invitation which, through the
power that accompanies it, *calls* men out of darkness
into marvellous light; from being aliens and foreigners
to become fellow-citizens of the saints and of the
household of God; from a state of willing darkness
and ignorance without, to that of accepted inquirers
and learners and disciples within ?

It may be said that these remarks are general and

indefinite, and that they need farther explanation. Let us seek that explanation in a part of the Word of God wherein the subject is discussed, in contemplation of that view which is now open before us, and so approach to the application of it which I especially propose to myself this morning; I allude to the fourth chapter of the Epistle to the Ephesians.

There we learn respecting the Church, the following leading truths.

For the Church herself, *in view of the Divine purposes* for which she was instituted in this world, the apostle there instructs us that

There is one only visible *body* (I refer to the fourth verse), of which Christ himself is the Head. That Church may contain many recognized divisions, but still is the truth asserted: " As the body is one and hath many members, and all the members of that body being many are *one body*—so also is Christ." (1 Cor. xii. 12.)

Then this one universal body is pervaded by *one only Spirit*—the one source of spiritual life and energy and sympathy; producing every where and in all the same manifestations and fruits of holiness and love.

And to this one holy society, so united in all which is visible and all which is invisible, there is *one hope*, one ultimate expectation from their obedience to that calling which brought them into the number of God's people. They all depend on the same grace, and all anticipate the same eternal glory; therein still to be one undivided Church in Christ for ever.

In view of that CALLING which is the function of the Church for the " increase of the body," we learn in

the fifth verse of the chapter before us, that There
is *one Lord*, who is exalted to be Head over
all things; who sends forth his servants into the high-
ways to compel men to come in; by whose authority
they address their call to mankind, and by whose grace
that call is made effectual.

And the terms, we farther read, at once of the
ministration on the part of those who are appointed to
teach, and of obedience on the part of the hearer, are
one and the same. Even before the canon of Scripture was complete, one rule of *faith* prevailed in the
Church, which had been delivered by apostolic men,
and deposited in the records of each congregation; and
that faith, in its elements, was offered generally to mankind, and became the one universal condition of their
being received into the Church.

And for that privilege, there was but *one Baptism*,
in profession of the same faith, "in the name of the
Father, and of the Son, and of the Holy Ghost." So
believing and so baptized, they who were obedient to
the heavenly calling were born again into the Church,
and their reception was sealed by the one pervading
Spirit of that holy and elect body.

The apostle having so spoken of the unity of the
visible Church, both in her vital structure and in her
ministry of the truth to others, for the increase of her
society, through the heavenly calling, proceeds next to
trace her communion with the Father of all, for her
edification to eternal life, and the enjoyment of his
presence and glory in heaven.

The *one* Holy Spirit and the *one* Lord and Saviour
have been mentioned. The conditions of Baptism,

however, have not thus far been fully asserted. He adds, then, that to this Church universal—in heaven above and throughout the world in which we live— there is *one* God and Father of all, whose divine love first originated the great scheme of the salvation of the Church, whose wisdom accompanied its development, whose glory is manifested in the midst of the saved in heaven, and who still overrules and directs all to the fulfilment of his purposes in the Church, in her preparatory and militant state, in the present world: for there he dwells in the holy body; is present in all her institutions; ministers grace in all her services; and makes the visible society of his redeemed people his habitation.

From this point, in the striking chapter before us, the apostle speaks more particularly of the other, and it may be termed proper, end of the divine institution of the Church—the EDIFICATION of her members in preparation for her eternal inheritance.

And on this subject he would seem to take it as for granted, that "the *edifying of the body of Christ*" must take place through the Divine blessing on the instruction which should be given to them, according to the one changeless faith, and through the discipline by which that instruction is made practical and enforced. The perfecting of the saints is here said to take place through teaching; and all the divinely-appointed institutions of the Church are plainly implied to have this in view.

Men have been admitted into the Church by Baptism, on their profession of the elements of a true faith, whose foundation-principle is in the doctrine of the ever-blessed Trinity. In the particulars of that faith, so far as they are revealed, from the infancy and ignorance of their New Life, must the Church undertake to instruct them; that, daily, and to the term of their earthly life, they may grow in grace as they grow in the knowledge of our Lord and Saviour Jesus Christ.

Then, for this end, (I refer now to the 11th verse,) different orders of men were divinely appointed within the Church, who might at once devote their whole time to the work of the ministry, and also, according to their measure and office, receive of God grace for the efficiency of that in which they wrought for the instruction and edification of the Church. To some the Lord gave, not the office alone, but *the grace* of apostleship; to others, that of prophets; and in like manner to the rest. The God of order thus made use of one of the confessed principles of his own divine nature, for the restoration of fallen man to his own image and glory.

The next step in this wonderful economy, and the last to which I shall find it needful to refer, is described in the sixteenth verse. For the purposes of order, rule, discipline and instruction, it has appeared that it pleased God not to step aside from the types which he had impressed on all sentient and all intellectual nature, and which he had brought out in broad relief in the earlier, but the true though typical Church of the Jews, and, as it were, to create in its stead a democracy in the Christian society,—but he fixed the divine discipline and appointed the gradations of rule—powers which should be—to which the Church should render respect, and from which she should

look for instruction and guidance. It appears, however, from the verse before us, that although, for the
ends in view, suitable grace was bestowed on all the
various *orders of the ministry*, grace was not withheld
from even the meanest member of the sacred body.
The ministry were as the larger channels through
which the current of life first flowed for the nou-
rishment of the common whole;—they were the
branches connected with the great source of all
life. But the Divine purposes found not here their
limitation. The same stream of life, imbued with
adequate grace, flowed also and continuously through
every member of the body, and for the same purposed
end. "From whom the whole body, fitly joined together and compacted by that which every joint supplieth, according to the effectual working in the measure of every part, maketh increase of the body, unto
the edifying of itself in love."

And we here approach, as you perceive, the immediate purpose of my discourse.

But before I enter upon it, suffer me to occupy
your attention for a few moments on a subject which,
although apparently but collateral to it, is yet in our
day of the utmost moment, for serious consideration.

A long train of events, not difficult to be traced,
has happily led thoughtful men to meditate patiently
on the Divine purpose in the establishment of a
Church among mankind;—on her structure and her
uses;—and very especially on the claims of the
Church of England to be an integral part of that
Divine economy for the salvation of mankind. To
minds so occupied, with the Bible and the history of

the Church open before them, it was impossible that any other conclusion should arise but this—that the belief of a right doctrine is to be made effectual of the promised end in this world, as preparatory for the next, through the administration of a right discipline; that one chief end of faith as a practical principle, is the sanctification of the heart and the renovation of the life of him who believes; and that as men are not left to believe what their reason may seem to discover or their tastes to approve, so no more is the progress of edification after an order which human beings may choose to construct for themselves.

These are safe rules; and to these and much more in their particular development, we owe, in part, the more awakened attention of Christians in the present day to certain persons of acknowledged talent, information and piety in one of our Universities.

To the persons to whom I refer, with many who have associated themselves with them, I say we are indebted for the more marked awakening of our attention to the points at which I have hinted—to the *structure*, the *obligations* and *authority* of the Church;—to the *promised* efficacy of the Sacraments;—to the apostolic commission of which the ordained ministry, in a subordinate measure, partakes;—to the primary aid which we derive from the records of the first ages of the Church, preserved by the Fathers as *witnesses* of the truth of the Inspired Volume;—to the necessity of obedience to the orders of the Church;—and especially of effectual and persevering self-denial for the subduing of the flesh;—and the rest.

But it is deeply to be regretted that, altogether and

doubtless sincerely professing the contrary, there are not wanting among them those who do yet, in truth, approach, in some instances, with almost childlike temerity, the very precipice of *Romish error*, and want only, it would seem, the recklessness to take the last step which separates them from the gulf below. That these persons deny the sufficiency of the Scriptures, and look by way of *increase* to saving knowledge, not for the *witness* of divine truth—for which they may justly and well look, in the earliest records, but for the *opinions* of the Fathers,—men of like passions and tendency to error with ourselves;—that they attribute to the Sacraments a *necessary grace,*—not in view of the *promise* which is fulfilled immediately by God who gives,—not in view of the faithfulness of the receiver,—but in view alone of *the ministration* by him who is appointed to that office;*—that

---

* Is it scriptural, moreover, and according to the doctrine of our Church to say, as some do affirm, that the grace of the Sacrament is "supernatural grace," in any other sense than as all divine grace is "supernatural"? The next step is only after the ordinary mode and tendency of human error. "What is the meaning of the popular phrase, 'The Age of Miracles'? Is not every age of the Church an age of miracles? Is there *all* the difference, or, indeed, any thing more than the difference between things seen and unseen, (a difference worth nothing in faith's estimate,) between healing the sick and converting the soul; raising man's natural body, and raising him in Baptism from the death of sin? Is the wonder wrought at the marriage of Cana a miracle, and the change which the holy elements undergo as consecrated by the priest, and received by the faithful, no miracle, simply because the one was perceptible to the natural eye, while the other is discerned by the spiritual alone? Protestants must take care what they are about when they speak at random against the Church of Rome, lest they pave the way for things as far worse than Popery as irreligion is worse than superstition; first

they claim for the priesthood in absolution, not only the *declaration on authority* of the readiness of God to forgive, but a very part in the ministration of that forgiving grace, as bestowed in virtue of their office;—that they purposely withhold from the people the clear statement of the great fundamental doctrines of our religion, and would preach in measured and veiled terms even the cross of the Redeemer;—that they affirm that sin after Baptism is in a high sense unpardonable;—that they exalt the Church to the neglect of the Saviour;—that they justify, in some form, prayers for the dead;—that they seek to restore to our churches symbolical representations, and ceremonial observances which, as in former times, must again, if adopted, " give occasion to many superstitions;"*—but, above all, that they darken and render

rationalism, and next infidelity." See British Critic, Number LIV. p. 260.

* A diligent, careful and affectionate, but unprejudiced study of early Ecclesiastical History, by all who wish well to religion, and to whom it has pleased God to grant the opportunity for so doing, is at all times desirable and important, and, perhaps, the more especially so in the present crisis of the Church. But, we must bear seriously in mind that the Church has never been infallible, except as under the immediate guidance and authority of the Saviour himself and his inspired apostles. Romish errors have not been the only errors by which she has been from time to time polluted. In one view, then, we profitably study early Ecclesiastical History, when it is our especial aim to discover, not alone how the Church has guided herself in the purer ages of Christianity, but in what form, and how gradually, in points, perhaps, in the first instance, of very minor importance, but which eventually merged in the errors of Rome, she diverged in discipline and in doctrine from that which is plainly, and after the testimony of Holy Scripture, in accordance with the apostolic, and therefore divine model. Let us not lose or trifle with the experience of now more than eighteen centuries.

obscure, to say the least, the great doctrine of our religion, justification by faith alone;—that they assert and urge these and other like vain fancies, we regard them only as beacons to warn us of our danger;—we learn from their example, that an enlarged mind, extensive knowledge, and even sincerity and piety itself, will not preserve us from error when once we have diverged from the beaten path of the Word of God.

But I return to the point in my subject from which I digressed.

The one great object of the association and continued existence of the Church, is to render effectual of its purposes the economy of the Gospel for the salvation of mankind, first by the ministration of the Truth for the calling of men out of *the world*, and then *within* her own community, through the instrumentality of the appointed ministers, and through the common grace bestowed upon all her members.

Twice has *your* membership been asserted. You were *admitted* into the Church by Baptism;—your engagements and your blessings were renewed and ratified at your Confirmation. And now, in the presence of God and of each other, and in the presence, too, of those persons who are about to partake of the solemn rite, and may justly look to you for both an example and encouragement, I ask you, Have you stood to the covenant? Do you now stand to the covenant? Are you obeying the impressions naturally awakened in your minds by the events which are passing before you? and do you secretly renew your purpose, by God's help, to persevere in your fidelity to the end?

In view, then, of your Confirmation in the faith, privileges and obligations of the Gospel, still referring to what has been said, I proceed to inquire what is justly to be expected of you as a member, in the highest sense, of the Church universal, and then subordinately of the Church of England? I will hint only at a few of the heads under which this expectation would seem properly to arrange itself.

I. In the first place, the Church expects of you, *A growing acquaintance with the Holy Scripture, and a growing conviction of its supreme authority.*

It was after the reading of the law—all it commanded and all it promised—that the people of the Israelitish Church are said in my text to have *stood to the covenant.* The Church universal is the pillar and the ground of the truth as it is revealed in the Bible. All which restricts and all which adds to the written Word of God, and the authoritative revelation of his mind, is heresy or schism. The *call* of the Church is by the voice of the Word. The *edification* of the Church is based on the principles, doctrines, precepts and promises of that Word, and of these, in their order and bearing and place, that edification is properly the development.

The Church of England, too, as a part of the universal Church, demands the same of you. She uses the privilege accorded to her to make institutions and construct her services for *the edification* of her members; but her purity of faith and practice is in this, that she refers all to the Scripture, and uses the testimony of the records of the first ages of Chris-

tianity only as *witnesses*, of the first importance indeed, in the interpretation of the Word of God.

The Church of England has in her bosom some
who are cold, formal, political, and in other respects
unworthy members of her community. Why? Because
she has amongst her members those who do not personally and perseveringly give themselves to prayerful
study of the Word of God;—who do not "compare the
Liturgy with the Bible." If they loved and read and
prayed over the Bible more, they must love with con-
vinced and filial affection the services and the institutions of the Church of England for their good! Are
you then Bible-studying Churchmen?

Again, the Church universal and subordinately the
Church of England, of which you are confirmed members, expects of you,

II. *To concur cheerfully in her discipline, and
cordially to make use of her services, in view and with
earnest desire of the grace of which they are means.*

Observe the argument of the apostle in the chapter
of the Ephesians to which I have referred. Grace is
given to the ministry, and grace is bestowed upon
every member of the Church for the common benefit,
the universal and individual edification, of the body.

Again, then, I remark, that even though your life
be free from any gross manifestation of the dominion
of sin, yet if your religion be formal alone, and there
is no communication of vital principle and nourish-
ment to the understanding, the heart and the life,
through the services of religion, you obey not the exhortation of the apostle—" I beseech you walk worthy
of the *vocation* wherewith ye are *called*"—the calling

which, even formally obeyed, has made you a member of the visible Church of Christ. Away, then, with controversy—life affords not time for it—except where the subversion of error constitutes a duty of our profession. Let each man of you be deeply, sincerely engaged in rectifying his own deficiency of concurrence, for his spiritual good, in the institutions and services of the Church. Her very prayers both teach you the necessity of knowledge and faith and obedience and self-denial and love and hope; and they afford you the language most suitable for the expression of all. Let your spiritual life and your external religious conduct take their PRINCIPLES, indeed, as these take their principles, from the Word of God, but their *form* and *modes* of existence and expression from the guidance which the Church thus administers.

III. The universal Church primarily, and the Church of England subordinately, moreover, expects of you, *confirmed in her community, to be the means of the* COMMUNICATION *of the grace which you receive through her, to others.* The Church is *compacted* and *edified* " by that which every joint supplieth."

The chief offices of the Church we have seen are twofold, *calling* and *self-edification.*

And, now, is vital religion of so large influence on your heart, that you deny yourself, and earnestly and practically desire and pray and labour that through her appointed ministers the Church may be made in our day the instrument of the large diffusion of the knowledge and power of the Gospel *throughout the world?* I speak of the Church of England, especially in connexion, as it is, with a State which has now so large dominion, and therefore obligation as well as opportunity to fulfil what is thus enjoined on her. What do you individually supply towards this end?

Then, for your own *immediate neighbourhood—the baptized of this village*—the several officers of this parish—her men of business and her unoccupied residents—her heads of households—parents—children—servants—is it your sincere and practical aim—all confirmed as members of the Church of Christ—to diffuse through your own hearts and lives and energies and prayers, the principles and productiveness of an economy of grace? What are you supplying towards the compactness and growth and edification of that part of the body of Christ to which you belong?

And earnestly do I wish that this evidence of our communion were yet more manifest *in our public services*, when we meet together for the worship of God, —in prayer, praise, hearing of his word, and in the participation of the Sacrament of the Supper of the Lord. Bear in mind, then, that in the public ordinances of the Church, there may be many things expedient to order and discipline, which are only remotely connected with salvation. Even the rubrics of our Prayer-Book may be well studied and obeyed as formal aids to the common benefit of a congregation associated in worship—they may tend to *compactness* of the body, without otherwise affecting the interest of the life. Let there be unity of *modes* among us, even a hearty and universal response of Amen at the close of our prayers, as well as a unity of *faith*, of *love*, of *obedience* and of FORM. Ours is common prayer, worship in *common*—in communion, if you will. We meet not to hear another pray, but to join in prayer ourselves; not listlessly to pause while another reads, but to take part, to respond aloud, and so having fellowship and sympathy in the common emotions of the Church, at once to minister to and partake of the blessing which is desired and partaken of by all.

Then does the Church ask nothing of you in respect of those who are now about to be confirmed? Look to it, brethren;—so far as opportunity serves, again, I beseech you, aid privately in their instruction, and by diligence and prayer, according to your relationships, be desirous that they may be partakers of your grace.

IV. One other expectation does the Church indulge of those who have been confirmed. *She looks that in the use of her services and in the communion of her members, you be yourselves, collectively and individually, edified and built up into Christ the Head.*

Great privileges, of instruction, grace and devotional service, have you now, many of you for a long time, enjoyed as members of our apostolic Church. Do you render back the blessing which has thus fallen upon you?—a living, feeling, holy gratitude to the Giver of all good!

How does the Church give forth in her Articles the idea of her own community?

The visible Church of Christ is "a congregation of *faithful* men, in the which the pure Word of God is preached, and the Sacraments duly administered according to Christ's ordinance, in all those things that of necessity are requisite to the same."

When shall that idea be fulfilled? When shall we

recognize in our congregations, assemblies of faithful men;—true to their principles, and daily built up in their most holy belief through the privileges and obligations which belong to them;—daily, with *greater* earnestness of self-denial and prayer, as they have pledged themselves, renouncing the works and dominion of the devil, the pomps and vanity of the world, and the sinful lusts of the flesh;—daily *increasing in* the fixedness of belief in all the Articles of the Christian faith, and daily walking with *more* cheerful readiness and exactness of holy life in all the commandments of the law?

To you, my brethren, is the appeal now made. May God grant that it be not in vain!

The Word of God is freely opened before you. The Church points to that Word—explains its doctrines and enforces its obligations. You have professedly surrendered yourselves to her guidance, and claim to be obedient members of her community. What, then, is left to you but to keep ever in mind the vows of your infancy, and, till the stream of natural life shall cease to flow within you, to STAND TO THE COVENANT!

SERMON VII.

THE SACRAMENT OF THE LORD'S SUPPER

A MEANS OF GRACE

"GENERALLY NECESSARY" TO THE SALVATION OF THE CONFIRMED.

---

2 KINGS xxiii. 3:

And all the people stood to the covenant.

WHEN last I addressed you from this text, I had especially in view those of my congregation who were about to present themselves to the Bishop to be confirmed. The administration of that solemn rite has now taken place. More than ninety persons* were then admitted to a participation of the highest privileges of that holy community which is the body of which the adorable Saviour is the head—the one fountain of all grace—the source of eternal glory.

---

* It appears from the Register-books of this parish, that of those who have been baptized into the Church, and are come to years of discretion, only one-fourth of the males and one-half of the females present themselves for Confirmation.

With what feelings you then presented yourselves before the assembled congregation—with what deep penitence on account of your sins—with what sincere humbleness of mind—what confiding faith in the one great sacrifice—what utter renunciation of sin—what firmness of purpose to forsake, for the future, all worldliness, all vanity, all lusts of the flesh—with what prayerfulness and reliance on the Divine grace you determined for the rest of your life to present your bodies a sacrifice—reasonable, holy and lively, is known only to yourselves and to God. It becomes your ministers to hope the best, and diligently to provide that you be not without motives and instruction which may, by God's infinite mercy, dispose you to continue to the end in that path on which you have thus happily entered. I will endeavour, then, on the present occasion, to shew you, that as it is one of the greatest privileges and blessings granted to you, so is it a paramount duty arising out of your Confirmation, to partake of the Sacrament of the Lord's Supper; and that this privilege and duty is an effectual means of grace which can never be safely dispensed with throughout the course of your future life.

. If I detain your attention, in the first instance, on subjects which more than ordinarily demand thoughtful consideration, and if, moreover, I occasionally refer to statements already made in the course of my Sermons on Confirmation, look, I pray you, for the interpretation of my purpose in the truth, that there is demanded of us, as followers of Christ, a *reasonable* as well as a holy and a lively sacrifice in service,— and that there is in the present day, unhappily, on the

one hand, an impatience of all idea of efficacy in the
Sacraments beyond that of the ordinary means of
grace, and on the other, through fear of the evil consequences of laxity of principle on these subjects, a
tendency to the fatal errors in the contrary extreme,
invented and defended by the heretical Church of
Rome.

Various are the opinions which have from time to
time, and with various parties or individuals, prevailed in respect of this as well as of the other Sacraments;—that, for instance, the religion of Christ being
essentially a spiritual religion, all the ordinances of
that religion are merely spiritual, and therefore the
outward signs are not necessary to the Sacrament;—
that the outward signs, although necessary, are signs
only, calculated to aid in producing the effect of the
divine institution;—that in this form, in a limited
sense, it is only a feast of communion;—that, so far
from this being the case, those outward signs, though
still partaking of the nature of the elements, bread
and wine, partake also of the nature of the very body
and blood of Christ;—that, partaking therein, we do
in truth, in a sense in some sort natural as well as spiritual, eat his flesh and drink his blood;—that all this
is deficient of the Church doctrine on the subject,
which, say others, is this—that the bread and wine no
longer, after the consecration of the priest, retain of
their own nature, but become the very body and the
very blood of Christ; and that in the celebration of
the Lord's Supper, a sacrificial renewal of the offering
on the cross actually and effectually takes place, which
they, the Romanists, term the Sacrifice of the Mass.

What, then, affirms the Church of England on this interesting subject?

"The Supper of the Lord," she teaches in her 28th Article, "is not only a sign of the love that Christians ought to have among themselves, one to another, but rather is a Sacrament of our Redemption by Christ's death; insomuch that to such as rightly, worthily and with faith, receive the same, the bread which we break is a partaking of the body of Christ; and likewise the cup of blessing is a partaking of the blood of Christ."

"Transubstantiation," she adds, (or the change of the substance of bread and wine,) "in the Supper of the Lord, cannot be proved by Holy Writ, but is repugnant to the plain words of Scripture, overthroweth the nature of a Sacrament, and hath given occasion to many superstitions.

"The body of Christ is given, taken and eaten in the Supper, only after a heavenly and spiritual manner. And the mean whereby the body of Christ is received and eaten in the Supper, is faith."

Observe, then, the distinctive elements of this definition of the Sacrament of the Lord's Supper.

The Sacrament of the Lord's Supper, the Church seems to say, is truly a feast—a communion of holy love with the members of the Church of Christ, in participation of the effectual signs of our redemption— the broken body, and the blood which was shed, of the adorable Saviour—of participation, because we are blessed of God with pardon, and hope through the redemption of Christ, not only, as it were, by remote imputation, but by our being united with him, and so

made personally interested in the promises which are
in him yea and amen.   And the perfection of the
sign, she farther holds, is not solely in the eating of
the broken bread and the drinking of the wine.   As
both the one and the other, when consumed, minister
to the vigour, the health, the very structure of the
person, so the participation which they represent is, in
a heavenly and spiritual sense, intimate, healthful,
personal—personal in respect of each individual, and
in respect also of the communion of the Church as
members of the same body, one with another—of
which Christ is the Head, and therefore of all unitedly
with him.

And in all this the Church vindicates her definition of a Sacrament, which, she affirms, consists of two
PARTS—the outward and visible sign, and the inward
and spiritual grace, made one Sacrament by the grace
of the secret renewal of the covenant of pardon
through Christ, in which the soul is strengthened and
refreshed, and made fruitful to the glory of God and
to everlasting life.   The outward visible signs are
still the " creatures of God"—bread and wine.   The
inward and spiritual grace are, " the body and the
blood of Christ," in that spiritual sense in which the
Lord affirms, " I am the living bread which came
down from heaven: if any man eat of this bread, he
shall live for ever : and the bread that I will give is
my flesh, which I will give for the life of the world.
—Verily, verily, I say unto you, Except ye eat the
flesh of the Son of Man, and drink his blood, ye have
no life in you."   But because the Church intends to
imply no change in the elements, bread and wine,

through the consecration, or setting them apart for this holy purpose by the priest, she teaches us to believe that on our part the sacramental transaction takes place *through faith*, and the blessing is spiritually bestowed upon, and effectually received by, the believing—a faith which is of common efficacy to those who sincerely communicate in this Sacrament of the body and blood of Christ. To this subject we shall have occasion again shortly to return.

Meanwhile, it is needful to our present purpose to observe, that the principle which prevailed in the instruction given by the Saviour to his disciples, is for like reasons to be traced in the institutions which he formed for the establishment and edification of his Church. The elements, but not the development of all truth, were involved in that which he addressed to them, as he the more plainly affirmed in the instruction he gave to them on the very occasion when he first instituted this Sacrament: "I have yet many things to say unto you, but ye cannot bear them now. Howbeit, when he, the Spirit of truth is come, he shall guide you into all truth." That Spirit spake in the apostles and guided their minds in what they wrote, unfolding the truths which had been already spoken by the Lord, for the edification of the Church. To the Epistles, then, as explanatory both of the words of the administration and also of all which the Saviour had before uttered in remote and hidden reference to the subject, we must look for the larger understanding of our Lord's purpose in the institution of his Supper—how we are to explain more at large, that is, the transaction which is thus described: "As they were eating, Jesus took bread and blessed it, and brake it, and gave it to the disciples, and said, Take, eat; this is my body. And he took the cup, and gave thanks, and gave it to them, saying, Drink ye all of it; for this is my blood of the new testament, which is shed for many for the remission of sins."

As the Church, moreover, has professedly constructed her sacramental service, restricting the administration itself to the form used by the Lord, yet, on the whole, in the larger view of the farther development of the nature of the Sacrament, as the subject unfolds itself in the writings of the apostles, we may profitably occupy a few moments in directing our attention to a comparison of some of the doctrines which the Church has introduced into her service, with the statement of similar doctrines by either the Lord himself, or his immediate messengers of the truth. It is one step in commendation of the Church, if her apparent obscurities be in common with those of the Word of God.

We must restrict ourselves, in each instance, very shortly, to a few points.

I. In the first place, then, the Church lays down, as a first principle in the administration of this Sacrament, that "by Christ's meritorious cross and passion ALONE we obtain remission of our sins, and are *made partakers* of the kingdom of heaven:" for such ends, no room is left for confidence in the communion of either this or the other Sacrament. In like manner and in equally plain terms speak the Scriptures. "This man," they say, (Heb. x. 12—14,) "after he had offered one sacrifice for sins, for ever sat down at the right hand of God; for by one offering he hath perfected for ever them that are sanctified."

II. But the Church farther states, as a first principle in view of this ordinance, that God "hath given his Son our Saviour Jesus Christ not only to die for us, but also to be our spiritual *food* and *sustenance* in this holy Sacrament." "The cup of blessing which we bless, it is asked by the apostle, (1 Cor. x. 16,) is it not the communion of the blood of Christ?—the bread which we break, is it not the communion of the body of Christ?" which seems only an implied but authoritative explanation of the striking words of our Lord (John vi. 56)—"My flesh is meat indeed, and my blood is drink indeed: he that eateth my flesh and drinketh my blood dwelleth in me and I in him."

III. In near accordance with this, we find it asserted in our services, that as often as we partake rightly of this Sacrament, we are "partakers of his most blessed body and blood"—that is, partakers in the merits of his sacrifice. In like manner we read in 1 Cor. xi., after a simple statement of the mode in which the Sacrament was first instituted—"As often as ye eat this bread and drink this cup, ye do shew the Lord's death till he come:"* and this in intimate connexion with the previous recapitulation—"Take, eat; this is my body; this do in remembrance of me." "This cup is the new testament in my blood."

IV. Then we are taught to pray, in partaking of this Sacrament—"Grant us, gracious Lord, so to eat

---

* Comp. 1 Cor. xi. 26 and 27.

the flesh of thy dear Son Jesus Christ, and to drink his blood, that our sinful bodies may be made clean by his body, and our souls washed through his most precions blood, and that we may evermore dwell in him, and he in us." And how strikingly does the Word of God accord with all this! John vi. 53—58: "Whoso eateth my flesh, and drinketh my blood, hath eternal life, and I will raise him up at the last day; for my flesh is meat indeed, and my blood is drink indeed: he that eateth my flesh and drinketh my blood, dwelleth in me, and I in him: as the living Father hath sent me, and I live by the Father, so he that eateth of this bread shall live for ever."

V. The same striking passage involves in it the doctrine of the words in which the Church administers the sacred elements: "The body of our Lord Jesus Christ, which was given for thee — the blood of our Lord Jesus Christ, which was shed for thee—preserve thy body and soul unto everlasting life."

VI. But we are taught farther to profess our belief that those who have duly received these holy mysteries, being in common fed with the spiritual food of the most precious body of the Saviour Jesus Christ, are "very members incorporate in the mystical body of the Son of God, which is the blessed company of the faithful." And this, do not the Scriptures abundautly justify? Truly mysterious! "We are members of his body, of his flesh and of his bones." (Eph. v. 30.) "For as we have many members in one body, so we, being many, are one body in Christ." (Rom. xii. 4, 5.) Is this, then, connected with the subject before us? It is confessedly *spiritual* in its intention. Is it *sacramental* also? " The cup of blessing (I repeat the quotation for what follows) which we bless, is it not the communion of the blood of Christ? The bread which we break, is it not the communion of the body of Christ? For we, being many, are *one bread* and one body: for we are all partakers of that *one bread*." (1 Cor. x. 16, 17.) " My Father giveth you the true bread from heaven; for the bread of God is he which cometh down from heaven and giveth life unto the world." (John vi. 32, 33.)

VII. The Church, however, carefully guards us against the idea of a necessarily saving consequence from the participation of " the outward and visible part or sign" of the Sacrament. " The danger is great," she affirms, " if we receive the same unworthily: for then we are guilty of the body and blood of Christ our Saviour; we eat and drink our own damnation, not considering the Lord's body." This and the parallel passage of the Word of God mutually, indeed, explain each other: " Whosoever," saith the apostle (1 Cor. xi.), " shall eat this bread, and drink this cup of the Lord, unworthily, shall be guilty of the body and blood of the Lord; for he that eateth and drinketh unworthily, eateth and drinketh damnation to himself, not discerning the Lord's body." The Lord's body is therein truly, that is, sacramentally shewed forth; but he who believes not, does not recognize the symbol. Set apart, consecrated to this holy purpose, he desecrates and uses it for common ends. Appealing, as it does, to holiest emotions of the heart, he receives it in self-confidence, negligence, pride and unbelief, not discerning the Lord's body and the

Lord's blood. The most effectual of means of grace becomes thus to him a source of the deepest condemnation.

VIII. The strong language thus used by the inspired writer implies the importance of the subject, and the greatness and certainty of the blessing, as well as the high dignity which God himself has attached to this Sacrament where it is rightly received. We are therefore prepared for the counter assertion of the Church in respect of the *faithful* recipients: " The benefit is great if, with a true penitent heart and lively faith, we receive that holy Sacrament (for then we spiritually eat the flesh of Christ, and drink his blood; then we dwell in Christ, and Christ in us; we are one with Christ, and Christ with us.)" It is needless that I place beside this extract the parallel passages of the Word of God. To do so were only to repeat what has already been brought forward. The sacrifice of praise which is implied in the narrative, may sufficiently assure us of the conviction of blessedness in partaking of the sacred elements which possessed the minds of the first Christians. " And they continued steadfastly in the apostles' doctrine and fellowship, and in breaking of bread and in prayers, and, continuing daily, with one accord, in the temple, and breaking bread from house to house, did eat their meat with gladness and singleness of heart; praising God, and having favour with all the people."

But the subject here returns again to the point from which we digressed.

Thus much we have learned respecting the doctrine of Holy Scripture and of our Church, that our pardon

and acceptance with God are *alone* through the merits
and death of the Saviour, who became on the cross the
one only, full, perfect and sufficient sacrifice, oblation
and satisfaction for our sins; but that in partaking
rightly of the Lord's Supper, we do therein sacramentally, but spiritually and truly, so partake of the
body and blood of Christ, that as our bodies are nourished and preserved in life by the creatures of God—
bread and wine, set apart and consecrated to this end—
so our souls are, after a spiritual manner, nourished
and preserved in life by the body and blood of Christ,
and thus, he being in us, and we in him, our hope in
his merits and death is re-assured and confirmed;—that,
after the same mode, all the Church, rightly partaking
of the feast, have communion, through this mystery,
both with each other and with the Lord, sacramentally
confirming that unity which shall never be divided;—
and that all this sacramentally takes place, both individually and in common, through the immediate energy
of a living faith. " To such as rightly, worthily, and
with faith receive the same, the bread which we break
is a partaking of the body of Christ, and likewise the
cup of blessing is a partaking of the blood of Christ."

It is of the utmost importance, then, for us to know
what is the nature and range of that faith which is
productive of such great and mysterious results in the
participation of this Sacrament. The statement may
be made in few words.

It has sufficiently appeared that the effectual energy
of faith in the participation of the Sacrament of the
Lord's Supper, must be subsequent upon, or perhaps
rather arise out of, a simple reliance on the sacrifice of

Christ, without and antecedent to the Sacrament, for all pardon and all grace.

Thence arising, this energy of faith must regard, with an unhesitating confidence, the participation of the Lord's Supper as a means divinely appointed, peculiar in itself, and, to sacramental ends exclusive, of " strengthening" the bond of unity between the soul and Christ, for the ends of his great sacrifice, and refreshing it in that spiritual life which is to have its issues in eternity.

This sacramental faith must, moreover, have in it of the nature of holy and uniting communion with that of others of the faithful who partake therein, in view of that fellowship in which we are *spiritually*—that is, through the one Spirit (Eph. iv. 4) in the visible Church, in communion of the ONE BODY and, *sacramentally*, ONE BREAD in Christ.

Then, in respect of the nature of this faith, it is at once the most simple, the most large, and altogether *singular* and *exclusive* of all the energies of faith. There is this distinction between the operations of the imaginative powers and those of faith. The imagination gives a transient form to things which have possibly no existence—truth, that is, is *a mere accident* alone of what we imagine. Faith, on the other hand, realizes what is true ;—it is the evidence of things not seen, and the very substance of things hoped for. Truth, and the conviction of truth, and the realizing of the truth, are all *necessary* to the effectual, saving faith of the Christian.

Now, in many respects, all the energies of a true faith are alike ;—in some, where faith is *sacramentally*

called into energy, it is peculiar and exclusive. Faith
cometh by hearing, and then it is conversant with
those things, the truth of which rests on the authority
of God's Word, and is received by the understanding
and the heart. In the Sacrament, of which we now
more particularly speak, the Saviour has condescended
to make use of the subordinate operations of our nature.
Through what we hear, see, feel, taste, the truth is presented to us. The service in which we are engaged is,
like our own being, complex. The whole nature is
brought into the religious energy, and thus the sacramental act of faith is the concurrence—the submission
—the very eucharistical self-sacrifice of the faithful in
gratitude and love to the Saviour. "Here we offer and
present unto thee, O Lord, ourselves, our souls and
bodies, to be a reasonable, holy and lively sacrifice
unto thee;—humbly beseeching thee, that all we who
are partakers of this holy communion, may be fulfilled
with thy grace and heavenly benediction."

And here a very interesting and important question
presents itself to us. What is the place which the
participation of this Sacrament holds in the economy
of our salvation? The Church teaches, that, like the
others, it is " generally necessary to salvation." In
what view is this to be regarded as a truth?

In discoursing on the offices of the Church, we
observed that the institution and structure of that
holy body had chiefly two ends in view,—*calling* and
edification,—the calling of unbelievers into the faith,
obedience, privileges and society of the Church, and
the progressive edification of the saints. There are,
then, two Sacraments,—the one contemplating the

efficiency of the former of these duties, and the other attendant on and ministering to, whilst it seals and confirms the latter. The Sacrament of Baptism is the Sacrament of our calling into the Church. The Sacrament of the Lord's Supper is the Sacrament of our edification therein. The one is the Sacrament of our birth into the number of Christ's people, the other is the Sacrament of growth and increase in the divine life—our healthful progress towards the maturity of holiness and joy in heaven. The Sacrament of Baptism, *once* administered, is necessary to our new birth into the relationships, the privileges and the obligations of the family of the Saviour. The Sacrament of the Lord's Supper, *frequently* partaken, is necessary to the strengthening and refreshing and nourishing of our soul, through the personal and frequent renewal on our part of the covenant by which we surrender ourselves to the salvation which is alone by Christ Jesus. Baptism introduces us into the Church; but he who, though baptized, does not habitually partake of the Sacrament of the Supper of the Lord, is yet but at the threshold of religion—he is a babe in Christ— he hesitates at the very gate of the Church, and gives no promise that he will persevere to the end.

And do not such thoughts address themselves affectingly to you who have lately presented yourselves to the Bishop for Confirmation? You have proceeded farther than the first entrance of the Church. You have been instructed in the way of righteousness, and have openly declared your conviction of the truth of the Gospel—openly affirmed your determination, by God's grace, to renounce the world, the flesh and the devil, and to serve faithfully the Lord Christ. All this has been publicly acknowledged and ratified. The foundation is thus laid, and the building may from this time proceed. You are placed now among, not those alone who have obeyed the heavenly *calling*, but those who are henceforth to be *edified*, and built up with the body of Christ. The appointed sacramental means of this is the participation of the Supper of the Lord.

I. Very earnestly, then, and affectionately, in the first place, do I advise you, my young friends, to present yourselves to PARTAKE of this holy Sacrament. No injunction of our Lord is more definitely enforced than this—" Do this,"—eat this bread which is my body, and drink this wine which is my blood,—" in remembrance of me." Have your convictions led you thus far?—are you persuaded that the Gospel is true, and involves all your happiness in this world and all your hopes in another; and, for the attainment of these, that you must become and be acknowledged a Christian?—and shall your religion end there? This is manifestly one — the most affecting — the most effectual *means of grace*. But what intend we by this very commonly used term? A means of grace is a means by and through which the Holy Spirit influences the mind to its edification. To neglect wilfully, then, a means of grace, is to grieve the Holy Spirit of God; and to persevere in that neglect is ultimately to quench his kindly movements in the mind, and to drive him from us. You cannot—you ought not to expect to prosper as a Christian, unless you obey the Saviour's command in thus sacramentally appealing to him for his grace. You may, indeed, as alas! too many do, still cling to the name, regulate your life in some respects by the precepts, and hold the reputation of being a Christian; but in truth you will fall again, as they manifestly, in various measures, fall, under the dominion of the lusts of the flesh. You will give your heart to the world. You will be content, fearful self-deception! to live without God, and having no hope laid up for you in heaven! Far from you be all this! Rather henceforth " use all diligence to make your calling and your election sure." And as the chief appointed means, in connexion with others, of giving energy and success to your labours, gratefully associate yourself with the Church in this commemorative festival of love.

II. But, I pray you, approach that table in A PRE-PARED AND RIGHT SPIRIT. With a discriminating faith " discern" there " the body of the Lord." Think not of the bread and wine alone, but, solemnly and affectingly, of the very flesh and blood of the Saviour; and remember with gratitude the purpose of his sacrifice on the cross. In these things let your faith be alive and in energy when your lips press the signs of your redemption, and your heart is pouring itself forth in adoration and prayer.

And, to remember the meritorious blood-shedding of your Lord, is, in truth, to recall to your mind your own sinfulness and need of divine forgiveness. Be yours, then, a spirit of true penitence and humbleness of mind. Let your sins now pass in review before you. Though forgiven, for Christ's sake, let them never be forgotten by you—let them never cease to awaken regret in the deepest feeling of your heart.

Come, too, in peace with all mankind. "Forgive, and ye shall be forgiven." The spirit which harbours the seeds of hatred and vengeance against a fellow-creature, is not a spirit of prayer; it cannot be sacramentally engaged in the service of God.

And then, here present yourselves to God. At the table of the Lord repeat, in the secret chamber of your heart, all which on your part took place at your Confirmation;—renew your covenant with the Most High;—ask the fulfilment of all his promises to you in Christ;—resolve, as he shall assist you, to "lead henceforth a new life, following the commandments of God, and walking from henceforth in his holy ways."

We can never be worthy of, that is deserve, the blessings assured to us and conveyed by the Supper of our Lord, but we may partake of it and of them in a prepared and suitable state of mind—we may wor-thily, with a right faith, right views, a holy disposition and firm reliance on God's grace to enable us to be for the future obedient to his will, eat of that bread and drink of that cup.

III. I seriously advise you, moreover, to partake of that Sacrament NOW. Let not the present opportunity pass away from you unimproved. The feeling which disposes you to defer this duty, under the plea of fur-ther consideration, is a feeling of reluctance which will most probably issue in a total neglect of this divinely-appointed means of grace.

And observe, moreover, that now, for the first time, and by the especial direction of your Bishop who con-firmed you, an opportunity is afforded to you, in the administration of the Sacrament of the Lord's Supper, for giving assurance of your sincerity in all which you affirmed and took upon yourself at your Confirmation. Did you at that time ratify the promises of your Baptism, appealing for aid to the grace of God? Behold in this sacred ordinance an offer and a pledge of that grace! The solemn declaration—the affecting appeal—have scarcely passed from your lips, and will you already hesitate to make use of the privileges which have been granted, and determinately to follow out the professions of obedience which you have so freely made? Not my fears, for I have as yet no reason to doubt your sincerity, but my anxious desire that you should continue in the word of your Saviour, and shew yourselves to be his disciples indeed, thus plead with you. I pray you now to bind yourselves by yet stronger obligations to his service, through a public participation of the Sacrament of his body and blood.

IV. But, in the last place, my desire for the promotion of your spiritual and eternal welfere through the use of this appointed means of grace, does not limit itself to your attendance on the present occasion.

I exhort you very FREQUENTLY to be a participator of that holy Sacrament. It is effectually a Sacrament of renewal. Such is the "fault and corruption of your nature," that you are subject to a ceaseless tendency to suffer thoughts of your Saviour to slip from your mind, and, with him, to cease to remember the bond of gratitude, love and obedience which you so deeply owe to him, and which has now lately been solemnly confirmed. Pass, then, for the future, a life of habitual self-government and self-examination.

Close not your eyes against your own infirmities. Suspect the influence of all events on your religious feelings, purposes and character. Be willingly sensible of your need of the frequently repeated renewal of an impression of the obligation of the Gospel on your mind, and of the grace which can alone make such an impression effectual of its proper ends. And gladly let it thus be "known and read of all men," that, whatever others may choose, you have determined to serve the Lord!

Happy for us will it be, when this short life, with all its cares and responsibilities, shall have passed, if it shall be found that, having been introduced into the Church of Christ by THE SACRAMENT OF BAPTISM, ratified our solemn pledge at CONFIRMATION, and frequently sought the grace of God, and renewed our humble claim of his mercy in Christ Jesus, and our willing and cheerful surrender of ourselves to his service in the SACRAMENT OF THE LORD'S SUPPER, we have throughout, and to the end, "stood to the covenant!"

THE END.

Lightning Source UK Ltd.
Milton Keynes UK
UKHW022208021218
333278UK00006B/490/P